100 WAYS TO WIN

100 WAYS TO WIN

LITTLE ANSWERS TO LIFE'S BIG CHALLENGES

NIGEL CUMBERLAND

First published by John Murray Business in 2025
An imprint of John Murray Press

1

A CIP catalogue record for this title is available from the British Library

Hardback ISBN 978-1-52939-0-353
ebook ISBN 978-1-52939-0-377

Typeset by KnowledgeWorks Global Ltd.

Printed and bound in Great Britain by Clays Ltd, Elcograf S.p.A.

John Murray Press policy is to use papers that are natural, renewable and recyclable products and made from wood grown in sustainable forests. The logging and manufacturing processes are expected to conform to the environmental regulations of the country of origin.

John Murray Press
Carmelite House
50 Victoria Embankment
London EC4Y 0DZ

John Murray Business
123 S. Broad St., Ste 2750
Philadelphia, PA 19109

John Murray Press, part of Hodder & Stoughton Limited
An Hachette UK company

The authorised representative in the EEA is Hachette Ireland, 8 Castlecourt Centre,
Dublin 15, D15 XTP3, Ireland (email: info@hbgi.ie)

This book is dedicated to my son, Zeb, my stepdaughter, Yasmine, and to all those wishing to live life to the fullest.

'Open your eyes to the amazingness of life.'

Contents

About the author

Nigel Cumberland is the co-founder of The Silk Road Partnership, a leading global provider of executive coaching and leadership training solutions to some of the world's leading organizations. He has lived and worked in locations as diverse as Hong Kong, Glasgow, Budapest, Santiago, Dubai, Singapore, Guatemala City, Kuala Lumpur, London and Shanghai. Through his career he has gained the experiences and wisdom that have helped teach him what it takes to succeed and be highly productive in all aspects of his life and work.

Previously, Nigel worked as a multinational finance director with Coats plc, as well as for some of the world's leading recruitment firms including Adecco. He is a Fellow of the UK's Chartered Institute of Management Accountants. He co-created an award-winning recruitment firm based in Hong Kong and China, which he later sold to Hays plc. Educated at the University of Cambridge, UK, Nigel is an extensively qualified executive coach and leadership training professional. In 2016 he was made a Freeman of the City of London.

He is the author of a large number of self-help and leadership books, among which the most recent are: *100 Things Productive People Do: Little Lessons in Getting Things Done* (Nicholas Brealey Publishing, 2022), *100 Things Successful Leaders Do: Little Lessons in Leadership* (Nicholas Brealey Publishing, 2020), *100 Things Millionaires Do: Little Lessons in Creating Wealth* (Nicholas Brealey Publishing, 2019), *The Ultimate Management Book* (John Murray Learning, 2018), *100 Things Successful People Do: Little Exercises for Successful Living* (John Murray Learning, 2016), *Secrets of Success at Work: 50 Techniques to Excel* (Hodder & Stoughton, 2014), *Finding and Hiring Talent in a Week* (John Murray Learning, 2016) and *Leading Teams in a Week* (John Murray Learning, 2016).

Nigel is married to a wonderful woman named Evelyn, who spends her time as an artist. He has two inspiring children – a son, Zeb, and a stepdaughter, Yasmine.

Introduction

'Are you ready to kickstart your life?'

Welcome to *100 Ways to Win: Little Answers to Life's Big Challenges*, your guide for creating a fulfilling and successful life. If you've already read my earlier book *100 Things Successful People Do: Little Lessons in Successful Living*, I'm delighted to see you back. If you're new to reading my words of wisdom, a warm welcome.

Setting the stage

Take a moment to reflect upon what winning means to you. The answer will be as unique as your DNA since winning isn't a one-size-fits-all concept. Instead, it's based on your aspirations, dreams and goals, reflecting the intricate make-up of your own needs and desires. Whether you seek professional highs, rewarding relationships, good health, or simply some inner peace, let this book serve as your compass, designed to successfully navigate you through life's ups and downs.

In this book, you'll discover a collection of advice, tips and insights curated to help you unravel how to overcome whatever challenges and opportunities cross your path. From your boldest ambitions to your daily routines, each entry is crafted to energize you in every aspect of your daily life. Treat this book as your toolkit for moulding the life you envision – one small win at a time.

Your personal success menu

Before jumping into the 100 entries, let's take a moment for some self-reflection: What does winning really look and feel like for you? Is it having that coveted corner office with a beautiful city view, creating a healthy and active lifestyle, developing important relationships, achieving financial independence, maintaining calm and peace, or perhaps achieving a balanced blend of all these wishes? The possibilities are as boundless as your imagination and they're likely to evolve as you experience life's twists and turns.

The big challenges you wish to overcome probably fall into one or more of these areas:

- Career and work
- Relationships and family
- Personal development and character building
- Financial stability
- Physical and mental well-being
- Lifelong learning
- Retirement and legacy

This book covers all of these. You can treat it like a menu of possibilities, offering a selection of ideas and activities to cater to every occasion.

Navigating the 100 ways

Within these pages, you'll encounter 100 succinct yet impactful entries, each one presenting a fundamental concept for you to explore and practise. The first page of each chapter reveals the importance of the idea, exploring why it's integral to your journey. The second page lays out some actionable tips and advice. View this book as your personal coach and mentor, distilling decades of experience and knowledge into practical steps tailored to you and your journey.

Some of the exercises and activities may feel familiar, serving as friendly reminders to do the right thing. Others will be new, launching you into uncharted territory. Embrace them all. They are your springboard to forming new habits and behaviours, cultivating fresh mindsets and thinking, to accelerate you towards winning success.

The coach behind the words

Let me share a bit about myself. I'm a successful life, leadership and career coach and mentor and I've had the privilege of guiding diverse individuals located all over the world. The insights presented in this book are distilled from the collective wisdom gained through my hundreds of coaching engagements.

In addition, during my life spanning half a century, I've been blessed with various achievements:

- a loving marriage and time as a parent
- academic achievements, including studying at the University of Cambridge
- a dynamic career trajectory, reaching the position of a regional finance director in my twenties
- a globe-trotting existence, living in over eight countries and working in at least 50
- entrepreneurial endeavours, including co-founding and later selling on a successful recruitment company
- an established presence as an author and speaker
- a passion for coaching, manifested through my business, The Silk Road Partnership
- most importantly, a sense of awe and peace with the life I've crafted and the person I've become.

A final and very important source of my wisdom has come from the many low points and disappointments I've faced – failed business start-ups, career struggles, relationship woes and inner struggles, to name just a few.

Your journey begins now

The ideas and activities you'll encounter in the following pages are not just concepts to learn; they're the keys to unlock life you deserve – one filled with purpose, enrichment and triumphs.

Start your exploration of *100 Ways to Win* with the confidence that each turn of the page will bring you closer to unveiling the extraordinary life that awaits you. May your journey be as transformative for you as it has been for countless others. Here's to your winning ways!

BE UNIQUE

'Show the real you in a world that encourages conformity'

The pressure to conform to other people's expectations is deeply ingrained. It starts in childhood and never lets up. We're all shaped by the people around us – parents, siblings, classmates, teachers, colleagues – and we all have a natural desire to please and be accepted. It plays out every day in your political views, your fashion choices, the career path you've chosen, the way you decorate your home and the car you drive (or your reasons for not driving a car).

None of this is bad in itself but it becomes problematic when your choices conflict with your values, desires, needs and ambitions; when decisions are made to please others, rather than coming from your authentic self.

If you're not careful, you can be so busy conforming to expectations, you can actually lose *yourself*.

When you reject the path of conformity, two magical things happen. Firstly, the pressure to be something you're not evaporates, leaving you with the joy of being true to yourself. And secondly, you'll discover that the people who matter love this new authentic you.

And that's a winning formula.

It's time to stop blending in with the other sheep and instead allow the real you to shine through.

Put it into action 1

Embrace your uniqueness

Being the real you requires a shift from *externally* driven choices to decisions that resonate with your own feelings and aspirations. These steps will help you make this shift:

1. Pause and evaluate whether the choices you make stem from genuine alignment with your values, or if they are motivated by external expectations and pressures. Practise only doing things that come from your heart rather than from your brain – what you *think* you should be doing.
2. Identify those activities, subjects or pursuits that you're genuinely passionate and excited about. Engage fully in these, even when others around you are doing something else.
3. Think through your personal values and principles. Use these to guide your decisions and choices, rather than allowing other people's preferences to dictate yours.
4. Have the courage to express your opinions and thoughts, even when they differ from those around you.
5. Finally, celebrate being different and understand that we all have unique needs, wishes and preferences, even if most people keep their uniqueness hidden.

AUDIT YOUR HABITS

'Clean up your act if you want to succeed'

Habits are the building blocks of success. Get them right and you've cracked the winning code. What could be more powerful than having a set of ingrained positive behaviours regularly nudging you in the right direction? It's you on autopilot, constantly correcting your course and steering you towards the wins in life.

Good habits smooth your path to family harmony, career success and personal fulfilment, but unhealthy ones block the flow. We all have them – good and bad – we just don't always recognize them. We're going to put that right now, because winning isn't just about doing the right things well, it's about *stopping* doing things that are holding you back.

Take a moment to write down the bad habits you have in each of these areas. On the next page we'll start cleaning them up.

- Sleeping and resting
- Eating and drinking
- Exercising
- Looking after your body
- Reading and learning
- Saving and investing
- Problem solving
- Giving back to others
- Communication style
- Teamwork

Holding onto your bad habits will only hold you back from achieving your full potential.

Put it into action 2

Identify what needs cleaning up

Did you find it easy to list your unproductive habits? It's often those things you feel guilty about not doing well, like not exercising regularly or eating unhealthily. If you're not sure, ask your family, friends or colleagues for things you should stop or start doing, or do differently. They'll be able to offer you some very helpful, objective tips.

Commit to change

We're all creatures of habit and changing what we do isn't easy. It's a lot easier to stop doing a bad habit if it's causing you discomfort or pain but the downsides aren't always immediately obvious. Try to see the bigger picture and identify those habits that seem innocuous that could in fact be holding you back. This should serve as a wake-up call to sort out your unhealthy behaviours.

Create consistent replacement habits

Consciously choose positive habits to replace the bad ones. This could be as easy as exercising more or picking up a book. You'll find lots of positive habits and behaviours in the following pages with specific help and advice on how to adopt them.

Celebrate milestones

With any habit you want to stop or change, give yourself an incentive. So, for example, if you've successfully not eaten junk food for a month, celebrate that. Have someone hold you accountable for changing a habit and celebrate together when you've made a breakthrough.

Maintenance is key

Cleaning up your act isn't a one-off process. You need to reflect regularly on which of your habits are helping you achieve a healthy and balanced life and which are working against you. Keep a 'to-be' list which you regularly update (see No. 36 to learn more).

BEFRIEND YOUR EMOTIONS

'Get your emotions working for you, not against you'

Flourishing careers and relationships can crumble due to lack of emotional maturity. Whether you call it poor emotional intelligence or a low emotional quotient, or EQ, there's a lot of it around. Have you ever:

- reacted impulsively to an email, hitting 'reply all' and unleashing your anger?
- raised your voice during a team meeting when faced with disagreements?
- responded to a partner's forgetfulness by giving them the silent treatment?
- succumbed to jealousy when a colleague secures a promotion over you?

This is known as being 'triggered' – when you allow your emotions to take control, especially in moments of distress, shock, stress or surprise. An immature response can set off a chain reaction, where your triggered state prompts those around you to respond in the same way. The repercussions can be severe – from fiery arguments and fractured relationships to job losses and marriage breakdowns.

Tame your emotions and use them optimally to help you succeed.

Put it into action 3

Pause your trigger

Think about being triggered by other people as learning to handle a firearm, where an instructor insists that you silently count to five and question *why* you're pulling the trigger before you do. When you feel triggered, pause, acknowledge your feelings and resist the urge to act impulsively.

- If you feel yourself getting angry during a meeting, just excuse yourself and go and take a few deep breaths.
- If you've had to write a difficult email, just pause before sending it. Save it in your drafts, step away from your device and reread it later when you'll probably find you have enough distance to adjust the tone.
- If your partner's upset that you've forgotten a significant event, apologize and listen. Never make excuses.

Always grant yourself the time you need to regain your composure. Healthy self-management might involve closing your eyes, counting to ten, taking a short walk and asking whether it's the authentic you who wants to shout, or your bruised ego.

Never use emotional reactions to win an argument. Don't act like a victim or deflect blame. After silently reflecting on your emotions and their origins, plan a mature and composed response. To be clear, anger or upset are sometimes warranted, but normally responding based on facts and without emotion is the best response.

MAKE SACRIFICES

'Look for what you need, not just what you want'

Life is a series of continual choices, because you can't have everything all at once. There's never enough time, money or resources. Life requires constant decisions around sacrificing one thing for another:

- Get a job or go to university?
- Stay single or tie the knot?
- Work fewer hours or earn more for a holiday?

Some choices are straightforward, but others involve choosing one option over another. The most demanding sacrifices often involve delayed gratification; giving up an immediate pleasure for future gains, such as passing up on a holiday so you can reduce your hours at work. It's not uncommon to feel stuck and to procrastinate in these situations.

How good are you at making the trade-offs life demands?

Making hard choices today can create an amazing tomorrow for you.

Put it into action

4

Be thoughtful

When confronted with an important decision, especially if it comes with competing choices, take your time. Ponder the implications of each option and think about the sacrifices you'll need to make. Be sure before committing.

Embrace delayed gratification

Always be willing to defer instant pleasure for future rewards, even when it feels really challenging.

If you're cutting back on luxuries to save for future endeavours, encourage those around you to do the same. Shared sacrifices are more bearable and the mutual support will help ensure you don't give up too easily.

Sacrifices are an inevitable part of life, but by approaching decision-making thoughtfully and embracing delayed gratification, you can navigate important choices with a greater sense of purpose and satisfaction.

LOVE YOURSELF

'Learn to accept yourself, even if you don't feel worthy'

One thing you can be sure of, you are your own harshest critic. I work with many successful people who are beset by doubts and insecurities; high achievers who have a remarkable capacity to find fault in everything they think, say and do.

Self-doubt, imposter syndrome, the urge to belittle yourself – these traits often originate in childhood or early adulthood, where negative messaging from parents, siblings, teachers, peers or caregivers can leave a lasting impact. The origins could be in bullying and name-calling by schoolmates, unconstructive comments from teachers, or lack of positive feedback from parents.

Failing to recognize and break unhealthy patterns can leave you with chronically low levels of self-confidence and self-belief, leading to a downward spiral which can impact your relationships, friendships, career, personal health and well-being.

Being kind and loving to yourself creates a foundation for a rewarding and fulfilling life.

Learn to authentically love yourself

The journey to self-love is an ongoing process of being patient and kind to yourself and seeing the positive qualities you possess.

- Take small steps and give yourself time, recognizing that valuing and loving yourself is a gradual process. Start by appreciating small aspects of what you are doing and achieving.
- Acknowledge all positive feedback when it is given to you and be open to receiving it from others. When praised, take a moment to recognize it and let it sink it. If a friend compliments you, thank them and take pride that you are indeed as good as they say you are.
- Talk positively to yourself. Remind yourself that you are not the sum of your weaknesses. Allow yourself to understand that your weaknesses, mistakes and flaws do not define you or your identity. They're only part of what makes you human along with your many strengths and positive qualities.
- Treat yourself to activities you love and that contribute positively to your well-being. Prioritize your own self-care, knowing that you are worthy and that you deserve to be kind to yourself.
- If unhealthy patterns do persist, consider seeking the support of a therapist or counsellor to help you work on your mental health. Suggested therapies might include cognitive behavioural therapy (CBT), which is sometimes the only way of breaking deep-rooted and detrimental habits.

STAY POSITIVE

'Prepare for the tough times and remember that the sun always rises'

If you tend to feel overcome with sadness when faced with terrible news, you're not alone. Most of us struggle to respond positively to difficult or negative changes and events in our lives. In the face of tragedy or unexpected losses, we typically find ourselves feeling a mix of anger, upset, confusion and denial.

How would you respond in any of these scenarios?

- During an economic downturn you're unexpectedly made redundant from a job you loved.
- A parent receives a stage 4 cancer diagnosis and passes a few weeks later.
- Severe injuries from an accident lead to a life-changing physical condition.
- AI changes the market and your business goes bankrupt.
- Your partner declares that they want a divorce and moves out of the family home.

Events like these can indeed 'break' you – draining your energy, pushing you into depression and leaving you unwilling to go out and face the world.

Remember, though, what doesn't break you makes you stronger. No matter how challenging the situation, life does go on, and while life goes on, the potential to regain positivity, hope and optimism remains. I speak from personal experience when I tell you that you can find light even after being lost in the darkest of tunnels.

When facing life's difficulties, always try to remember that things will eventually improve.

Put it into action 6

Allow time for healing

- Talk to people you trust and allow yourself to express your emotions. Know it's OK, and healthy, to cry as you open up and find comfort in the support of others.
- Give yourself time to grieve what you've lost or what has changed – the loss of a loved one, an opportunity, a job. Resist the urge to make rash new decisions to fill the void. Instead, practise patience.
- Emotional upheavals can drain you and maintaining your well-being and health is crucial. Perhaps you need more sleep, healthy comfort food or just silence. Do whatever it takes to look after yourself.

Recognize the impact on yourself

- Understand that the events you've faced will change you, and that's OK. You may become more cautious in future relationships or when job hunting. You'll hopefully also have a newfound appreciation for what you have, recognizing how easily things can be lost.
- Living through big shocks and challenges is an opportunity to grow and gain wisdom. It may take weeks or even months, but eventually, you will emerge stronger and wiser.

SPEAK UP

'Stand up for what is right'

Your voice matters. We all have views about what's happening in the world. We've all felt touched and inspired by the struggles and challenges people face – whether in our own backyard or on the other side of the planet.

The range of issues people fight for is vast. From LGBTQ+ rights and government corruption, to racism and environmental conservation, each cause is an opportunity for people to speak up and make a difference.

You can add your voice to anything that matters to you, no matter how personal or how much time has passed. Consider the #metoo movement, where sexual abuse survivors courageously spoke up after decades. You may choose never to be as vocal as Malala Yousafzai or Greta Thunberg, but, with your own perspectives and experiences, you have the potential to find your own cause and your voice.

Throughout history, impactful changes have been driven by those willing to speak up. Finding your voice can help contribute towards a better world.

Speaking up may be hard but is so much more rewarding than staying silent.

Put it into action

7

Discover your cause

- Some people discover their passions in childhood; other people take longer. Don't feel guilty if you haven't found your cause yet. Start listening to what makes you upset, or angry, or what you feel opinionated about. Make time to deep-dive into those issues and topics where you have opinions and feelings. Explore which of these issues you'd like to take action on.
- There are lots of ways to speak up – joining groups, participating in online discussions, signing petitions, contributing financially to causes or travelling to participate in demonstrations.

Overcome your hesitations

- Step out of your comfort zone and remember there's always a first time. Give it a try and learn as you go. Strength is found in numbers, so connect with like-minded individuals by joining groups or engaging in debates or protests.
- Start small, for example by subscribing to a newsletter or Facebook group.
- Schedule time in your diary for action, whether it's an hour a week exchanging views on an online forum or a weekend spent at a protest march.

GET OUT OF YOUR CHAIR

'Feel the energy'

We've evolved as creatures that move, but sadly today sitting down seems to be the primary way of life, whether that's in meetings or at a work station, watching TV or travelling by car, or writing a book (speaking from experience!)

Prolonged sitting saps your energy and vitality. It reduces circulation in your body, weakens your muscles, stiffens your joints and leads to higher blood pressure.

More than that, though, many of our mental activities don't flow well when we tackle them from a seated position, whether it's reflecting, brainstorming, thinking out of the box or managing conflicts. That's why I sometimes conduct my face-to-face coaching sessions while walking, rather than remaining seated for an hour or more.

So ditch the chair and the couch and feel the energy flooding back. The only thing you've got to lose is your lethargy.

Sitting down all day is a sure way of shortening your life span.

Put it into action

8

Be intentional about standing up

- Consider a standing desk, ideally one of those ones where the height can be controlled so that you can alternate between sitting and standing.
- Always take phone calls while moving around. You'll come across as more alert and less likely to be distracted by things such as what's on your computer screen.
- Give yourself reminders to stand up and stretch every hour to energize yourself.
- Walk for 30 minutes a day to enjoy an amazing impact on your wellbeing.

BE AN AMBIVERT

'Tap into the best qualities of introverts and extroverts'

Did you know that each of us is born either introvert or extrovert? That means you are either someone who quietly thinks things through before speaking up or who talks as ideas come into your head. The proportion of introverts to extroverts is roughly 50:50.

We spend our childhoods practising what is natural to us: a typical young introvert might be drawn to reading, thinking, being alone and staying quiet while their extrovert friends are constantly talking and interacting.

By the time you reach adulthood, you'll be perceived as either a shy listener and deep thinker, or a polished communicator who never stops talking. But just because we are born a certain way doesn't mean we can't cultivate other ways of being.

The secret to a successful life is mastering both qualities, so it's time to unleash your inner ambivert and enjoy the best characteristics of introverts and extroverts. If you can master this, you'll be able to switch between sharing ideas in the moment and confidently taking the stage, while also listening well and spending time alone reflecting and contemplating on issues.

To be successful in any setting, it's useful to be able to draw upon the skills of both extroversion and introversion.

For the introverts, take the floor

If you're an introvert, it's time to embrace the extrovert's skill of joining conversations and speaking up in any setting. Most introverts struggle with this and often stay silent. Try using 'filler sentences' to ease you into any ongoing conversation:

- 'If I can build on the ideas shared so far ...'
- 'Let me add my perspective to the discussion ...'
- 'Allow me to share some additional thoughts ...'

These phrases buy you a few seconds to help give your 'introverted' brain time to speak up; it gives you a moment to compose yourself before speaking.

And for the extroverts, try to avoid always sharing every thought that crosses your mind. Practise staying silent in meetings. This will enable you to listen and think, while giving others the space to contribute. When you do want to speak, ask yourself, 'Do I really need to be heard now?' This moment of reflection stops you being on autopilot and opening your mouth simply for the sake of it.

EMBRACE THE PRESENT

'Stop living in the past and worrying about the future'

It's easy to become entangled in the noise of the past or consumed by worries about the future. But the past is finished and the future is unknowable, so there's really only one sensible path and that's to ignore both of them.

Dwelling on your past, carrying regrets and being nostalgic about what has happened will only cause you to miss out on what's happening right now. Similarly, being preoccupied with your future and anxious about what may happen takes your attention and energy away from the present.

The present isn't just a meeting point between your past and future; it's the only juncture in your life where you can shape things, where you have what psychologists call agency. It's in the present moment that you make the decisions and choices that in turn will shape your life. As a result, much of your ability to create the life you want resides in what you choose to do and think now.

Think of present moments as your springboard to building a meaningful life for yourself and those around you.

An easy way to waste your life is to spend it living in the past or in the future.

Put it into action 10

Become more mindful of the present

Engage in activities that demand your full and undivided attention, forcing you to be in the present. This practice encourages your brain to focus on the here and now, redirecting your mind away from what's happened or what might happen.

Meditation is a proven method for achieving a heightened awareness of the present moment. If you're new to it, start by dedicating at least ten minutes each day to sitting quietly with your eyes closed, focusing on your breathing and allowing your thoughts to come and go without judgement or internal commentary.

To help keep your mind focused on the present moment, become more aware of what is happening around you – observe the rain hitting the ground, see how a gardener prunes their fruit trees, watch birds soaring above, or notice a window cleaner at work.

There are lots of immersive experiences that will help connect you to the present moment: try walking in nature, swimming, spending time with close friends, working out in the gym, or engaging in artistic pursuits like painting or writing poetry. Whenever your mind starts to wander from the task at hand, gently guide it back to the present moment. Tell yourself, 'Look at all those beautiful trees swaying in the wind' or 'Let me count my swimming strokes.'

DON'T HOLD ON TO HURTS

'Forgive people who upset you'

In life, you'll encounter people who stir emotions you'd rather not feel – anger, frustration, even hatred. It's easy to believe that holding on to negative feelings somehow affects the person who triggered them. The truth is, harbouring resentment is like drinking poison and expecting someone else to suffer. The impact is on you, not them.

When you cling to anger, you create a toxic environment within yourself. It clouds your judgement, taints your outlook and erodes your peace of mind. The weight of resentment only grows heavier with time, burdening you with unnecessary emotional baggage.

Why hold on to a poison that corrodes your own well-being?

Negative emotions consume your thoughts, affecting your mental and emotional well-being. And the irony is, the object of all this pain might not even be aware of your feelings. You're giving someone you don't value power over your own happiness and well-being. Holding on to anger is a self-imposed prison and the only one suffering is you.

No longer carrying the weight of anger, upset and bitterness will leave you lighter, more positive and energized.

Become expert at letting go

- Appreciate that everyone makes mistakes and the person who hurt you is human, just like you. We all carry burdens and flaws. Understanding this is the first step towards releasing the anger or upset you're holding on to.
- Practise forgiveness – this is not about condoning or forgetting the actions of others, but about empowering yourself to move forward. By letting go, you reclaim control over your own emotions and life, and you are no longer defined by the hurtful actions of others.
- Your mental and emotional well-being should be a top priority, so focus on self-care. Instead of allowing negative feelings to fester, redirect your energy towards activities and thoughts that nurture your growth and happiness.
- Break the cycle of resentment by replacing your negative thoughts with positive affirmations. This can be hard, but keep going. By actively steering your mind towards positive thoughts and feelings, you create a space where forgiveness and peace can flourish.

JUST WALK AWAY

'Give toxic people a wide berth'

Have you ever found yourself entangled in relationships or friendships that drain your energy, diminish your self-worth and sow seeds of negativity? It's crucial to recognize the profound significance of being willing to walk away. Life is too short to endure toxic relationships that hinder your personal and emotional well-being.

Unhealthy relationships take many forms – from draining friendships that offer little support, to romantic entanglements that sap your positive energy, to jealous colleagues who try to undermine you at every turn.

Acknowledging when a relationship has run its course and become toxic is part of becoming mature and wise. Walking away can be a powerful declaration of self-love and self-worth, leaving space in your life for healthier relationships to grow that will foster your growth and bring you more happiness and fulfilment.

Walking away from certain people can be really hard, but the benefits to your well-being can be enormous.

Intentionally decide to stay or to leave

- Know that it's OK to say, 'Enough is enough.' We all deserve relationships that allow us to feel safe, be ourselves and energize us. Understand that walking away is an affirmation of your self-worth and that you value yourself.
- Take a moment for some self-reflection and assess how a problematic relationship aligns with your values and contributes to your growth, as well as how it makes you feel. If it consistently hinders your well-being, it may be time to consider stepping away from that person.
- Before walking away, consider communicating your needs and boundaries to that person to give them a last chance to change. If the relationship persists in being unhealthy, establish firm boundaries to protect your own emotional and mental well-being. For example, if they are a work colleague, you might consider no longer socializing with them.
- To gain an external viewpoint, reach out to friends, family, or a trusted confidant to help you gain more clarity on how you're feeling about a toxic person.
- If necessary, plan how you will walk away. How you do this will depend on your situation. You may be able to simply stop taking their calls and replying to their messages. Or you may have to do something more drastic such as moving out of your home or quitting your job.

DO NOTHING – IT CAN BE GOOD FOR YOU!

'It's OK to stop being busy and do nothing'

In the hustle and bustle of our fast-paced lives, the idea of doing nothing might seem counterintuitive. We value active people and admire those well-known figures who always seem to be busy doing things and achieving, often in more than on area. Yet I have coached far too many people like this whose constant busy-ness has led them to burnout, stress and overwhelm. It hasn't brought them happiness.

This also applies even to us ordinary folk. Even if our day job isn't too demanding, the constant bombardment of stimuli from the digital world and our daily responsibilities can be enough to leave us feeling drained and depleted.

Doing nothing is a crucial aspect of self-care and embracing moments of stillness and allowing yourself to simply 'be' can be profoundly beneficial. Never think that doing nothing is a waste of time – it's an investment in your mental and emotional well-being. Just as a muscle needs rest to grow stronger, your mind requires moments of stillness to maintain clarity and focus.

> Sometimes the most productive solution is to do nothing.

Create moments of doing nothing

- Allocate specific time in your schedule for doing nothing. Whether it's a few minutes each day or a more extended period each week, make it a priority.
- Engage in mindful breathing exercises. Take slow, deep breaths, focusing your attention on the inhalation and exhalation. This simple practice can bring a sense of calm and presence.
- Turn off the radio, put away your smartphone and disconnect from the digital world. Allow yourself to enjoy moments without the constant buzz of noise and notifications.
- Spend time outdoors doing nothing more than taking a short walk in the park or sitting in your garden.
- At work, step away from non-important meetings, say no to non-urgent tasks and use the freed-up time to pause and be alone.
- Engage in activities that allow your mind to wander. Whether it's doodling, daydreaming, or exploring a creative hobby.

OPEN YOURSELF TO LOVE CAREFULLY

'Give yourself to others without losing yourself'

Love is a powerful force that has the potential to transform our own and others' lives in so many ways. There's an important proviso, though. Whether it's your partner, children, family, friends or close colleagues, loving others – with all that entails – can be both energizing and draining. The emotional investment we make in these relationships can sometimes feel exhausting, even if the rewards can be immeasurable. Loving others means opening yourself up to vulnerability as well as empathy and understanding.

The secret is not to sacrifice your own well-being and identity. Instead, it's about striking a balance between nurturing your relationships while preserving your own sense of self. This is because love, in all its forms, is a reciprocal process and maintaining loving relationships with others while meeting your own needs is a constant work in progress. It requires skills such as self-awareness, boundary setting and a commitment to your own growth.

We all need to love and be loved, while holding on to who we are.

Put it into action

14

Nurture your relationships mindfully

- With your partner, discuss and establish clear boundaries that respect each other's time, energy and personal space.
- Prioritize self-care as an integral part of your routine, ensuring you have moments of solitude as well as time to engage in activities you enjoy.
- Foster open and honest communication in your relationships, by expressing your thoughts and feelings while actively listening to the perspectives of others.
- Focus on the quality of your interactions rather than the quantity. Meaningful connections thrive on depth and understanding and this often means being ready to listen and to open up.
- Cultivate empathy and seek to understand the emotions and needs of those you love. This will help create a supportive environment for mutual growth.
- Embrace and celebrate the individuality of both yourself and others. At a practical level this means encouraging others' personal growth as they pursue their own passions and dreams.
- Love is a marathon, not a quick sprint, so be patient and intentionally nurture your relationships. Always allow for both ups and downs along the way.

In No. 44, I delve deeper into how to stay in a successful long-term relationship.

LISTEN TO YOUR HEART

'Find your own answers'

Your inner voice is an invaluable resource that's able to guide you through even the most complicated of life's decisions and dilemmas. Unfortunately, though, we often allow the noise of the external world to drown out this guidance system that lies inside all of us. But no matter what we call this inner guide – our gut, heart, intuition, instincts, sixth sense or inner compass – listening to it is an important and learnable skill when we are facing life's more difficult moments.

Perhaps you don't know how you feel about a current relationship, or whether you should move overseas for work, or accept that promotion with all those extra responsibilities? The answer: stop worrying, keep still for a moment and listen to your heart.

Your heart holds a reservoir of wisdom shaped by your experiences, values and authentic desires. When coaching people who are facing tough decisions, I always ask them to silently reflect upon what they *feel* is the right way forward. I might ask them to close their eyes and ask themselves what their gut feeling or intuition is telling them to do.

The inner answers you hear may not always align with logic, but they normally resonate with your deeper self. They often carry valuable information that can guide you in the right direction, and learning to acknowledge and embrace this internal compass will empower you to navigate challenges with more clarity and confidence. As you cultivate this skill, you'll find that your heart becomes an ever more reliable guide for you.

That quiet voice in your gut can provide answers that you'll never find on an internet search.

Put it into action

15

Practise listening to your heart

Learn to trust the immediate feelings or hunches that arise within you, paying particular attention to physical sensations. Your body often communicates what your heart knows. A sense of unease or discomfort can be a powerful guide that you shouldn't do something. Conversely, warm and positive feelings about a way forward can often be the proof you need that it's a good choice.

When faced with choices, consider how each option aligns with your fundamental values, beliefs and aspirations. Keep a journal to record moments when your heart speaks – moments that may come when you're in the shower, meditating, driving or walking ... or indeed at any time.

Look back at how your intuition helped you

Reflect on decisions where listening to your intuition led to positive outcomes. Similarly, recall situations where ignoring your intuition might have resulted in decisions you regret making. Use these lessons learned to help you overcome doubts about the importance of listening to your heart's wisdom.

LET OTHERS HAVE THE LAST WORD

'Learn to stop your ego being in control'

Stop being that annoying colleague or friend who always has to have the final say. This urge can be very damaging to your relationships, your collaboration with others and your personal growth. This need to be right and to 'win' arguments often arises from an immature ego, one driven by a desire for dominance or the need to always come out on top.

Occasionally it's OK to crave to be the one out in front, to prove a point, or to satisfy your desire to be right, but most of the time it isn't. And the last person who benefits from this is you.

Giving others the privilege of the last word can be very healthy and fruitful, since it demonstrates a readiness to listen, learn and appreciate the perspectives of those around you. By surrendering your desire to be the winner, you open the door to deeper trust and understanding. This will improve any atmosphere, whether at home or in the office, creating a space where everyone's voice feels acknowledged and where people will enjoy working and talking with you all the more.

Not having the last word leaves you wiser and calmer.

Let go of the need for validation

Understand that your worth isn't determined by having the last word and being right. Whenever you feel your ego bristling, repeat this mantra over and over: 'It's OK if I don't have the last word.' Freeing yourself from a need for constant validation allows you to show up as your authentic self. You can exchange ideas and opinions without having to worry about how you will come out the victor.

Give others the last word

Start to view conversations as opportunities to learn rather than battles to be won and adopt a mindset that values the exchange of ideas over personal triumph.

- Focus on understanding what others are expressing rather than on formulating a counter-response inside your head. When others have finished speaking, pause and allow their words to settle before jumping in with your points. A few moments of silence won't harm but will benefit your discussion.
- Recognize that everyone brings a unique viewpoint shaped by their experiences and there's value in exploring these differences. Look for and acknowledge the positives in their insights and perspectives.
- Prioritize empathy in your interactions by seeking to understand the emotions and intentions behind others' words rather than fixating on finding errors and holes in their argument.

In No. 25, you can explore the related skill of becoming a good listener.

DANCE THROUGH THE STORMS

'Stop letting external circumstances control how you feel'

Life is an unpredictable journey, often presenting us with storms – challenges, setbacks and unexpected twists. The ability to navigate through these storms is a skill that can be learned and practised. And, once acquired, it's a skill that will transform the way you respond to future setbacks and moments of adversity.

Most external circumstances, just like the weather, are beyond your control. It might be your employer going bankrupt, your partner getting sick, or travel delays at the airport. You cannot control what happens to you, but your response to adversity is entirely within your grasp.

We're all capable of developing a mindset that accepts with grace and resilience things we cannot control. While we recognize that (most) storms are temporary, we can make sure that we have the inner strength to endure with calm and dignity whatever hurricanes and thunderstorms come our way.

> Remain calm inside no matter the weather outside.

Put it into action

17

Develop a resilience mindset

- Cultivate resilience by viewing each challenge as an opportunity for growth, armed with the knowledge that you can almost always bounce back. Embrace the wisdom of the Serenity Prayer – 'Grant me the serenity to accept the things I cannot change' – and acknowledge that certain aspects of life are beyond your control.
- Don't allow negative thinking to dictate your emotional state. Always remember that we are not our thoughts. You can observe this when you step back from what you're thinking and watch how thoughts and ideas randomly come and go in your head.

Build a support network

Surround yourself with positive influences. This might be as a simple as supportive friends, family, or mentors who can provide support, guidance and encouragement to help you deal with your storms.

Take a few deep breaths before responding

In every situation, you always have the power to choose your response, but you must ensure you are doing so free of panic, anxiety or fear. When in the middle of a raging storm, try to find a quiet place and moment to mindfully pause and calm yourself – perhaps just by closing your eyes and taking some slow, deep breaths. Only then should you decide on how best to act and respond to the challenge.

BE HONEST ABOUT YOUR ADDICTIONS

'Find the courage to overcome your addictions, both big and small'

We all have our addictions. These can take diverse forms and be of various magnitudes, though it's essential to recognize that no addiction is too insignificant to address. From the obvious to the subtle, each addiction has its own unique impact on our performance, well-being and relationships.

Understanding the reasons for an addiction is a crucial step towards healthy personal growth. Often, our addictive habits serve as coping mechanisms, providing momentary relief from other underlying issues or stressors. Acknowledging these patterns allows us to work on ourselves and reclaim our autonomy. So, no matter what your addictions might be – social media, drugs, porn, or overwork, or less obvious ones like bullying colleagues or taking undue credit for other people's work – make time and find the courage to explore how you can overcome them.

We all have addictions, but not many of us will admit to them or work to overcome them.

Put it into action

18

Name your addictions

Awareness is the first step towards change, and being honest about your addictions is an act of self-empowerment. It's about acknowledging your vulnerabilities, understanding the sources of your behaviours and taking intentional steps towards creating a healthier set of new ones.

Spend time understanding the deeper reasons behind your addictions, exploring whether they're linked to stress, trauma or some other unmet emotional need. Try to pinpoint the situations or emotions that trigger your addictive behaviours. Do you turn to drink or porn when feeling overwhelmed or really stressed, for example? Addressing these root causes is crucial for lasting change. You may need a therapist or counsellor to help you get to the bottom of what is happening.

Take remedial action

- Seek to replace addictive behaviours with healthier alternatives – if you're addicted to overwork, establish boundaries and allocate time for rest and leisure; if you're spending too long on social media, try setting up a daily time limit on your phone apps and use the freed-up time for more relaxing or fruitful activities.
- Hold yourself accountable for your actions by setting realistic goals and monitoring your progress towards overcoming your addictions.
- Put a support system in place to help make the process of overcoming an addiction more manageable. Having someone to help hold you accountable and allow them to regularly check in with you might be essential to overcoming your issue. If needed, seek out the support of groups such as Alcoholics Anonymous.
- If your addictions are deeply ingrained, seek guidance from therapists who can provide tailored strategies to help you overcome them.

BE OPEN TO THE UNLIKELY OR 'IMPOSSIBLE'

'Be more open-minded about the things you see and hear, and even those you don't!'

In a world buzzing with information, it's easy to dismiss ideas that seem far-fetched or unconventional. But what if I told you that some of the most extraordinary breakthroughs in history were once deemed 'crazy' or 'impossible'? Think of the times when unconventional ideas have reshaped the course of history – the possibility of circumnavigating the globe and the existence of whole continents or the once-ridiculed notion that the Earth moves round the Sun, rather than the other way round. The unlikeliest of events or theories have often proven to be real ... and revolutionary.

The truth is, being open-minded is not just a nice-to-have quality, it's key to unlocking your untapped potential and discovering innovative solutions to your challenges. By being open-minded, you position yourself to see beyond the obvious, helping you develop your creativity and adapt to a rapidly changing world.

Being open-minded isn't about blindly accepting every idea. It's about acknowledging that the world is complex and that the unlikeliest of possibilities might just hold the key to your personal and professional success. So, next time you're presented with a 'far-fetched' idea, be open – you never know, it may well turn out to be an extraordinary discovery!

Being truly open-minded can leave you open to amazing discoveries.

Develop your ability to be open-minded

- Actively challenge and question your assumptions and preconceived notions. Regularly ask yourself, 'What if I'm wrong?' This simple question can open doors to new perspectives. To broaden your understanding, read different newspapers to gain different perspectives and engage in conversations with people from diverse backgrounds, experiences and beliefs.
- When evaluating ideas, seek evidence for those ideas rather than confirmation of your existing beliefs. Be willing to accept that the 'crazy' idea might have a rational basis.
- Curiosity and open-mindedness go hand in hand and I encourage you to approach life with the wonder of a child, eager to explore and learn. Foster an environment – at home and in your workplace – that encourages creativity, 'out-of-the-box' thinking and a mindset that challenges and subverts the status quo.
- Spend time reading and understanding historical examples where unconventional claims and ideas have proved to be true and/or became mainstream. This knowledge can help your brain realize that the seemingly impossible can be true.

NEVER GIVE UP ON TRUSTING OTHERS

'Learn to trust again, even after someone has broken your trust badly'

Trust is like an invisible thread that binds us together in our relationships – with family, friends, colleagues, neighbours and others beyond. It's a thread that can take time to grow and strengthen, but, once broken, can be very hard to tie together again.

We've all experienced moments of our trust being tested, lost or broken, perhaps because someone has lied to us, not followed through on a promise or not done what they said they would do. Our trust in others is always liable to be tested simply because we humans all make mistakes and sometimes let others down. We need to be humble enough to accept human frailty, understand that trust is always an ongoing project and not an absolute, and be willing to put in the work to keep on building it.

By learning how to trust again, even after a terrible act of betrayal, you develop a skill that can transform your relationships as well as your own inner peace and strength. It opens the door to the possibility of deeper, more authentic connections.

Trust is an important life-success ingredient – nurture it whenever possible.

Acknowledge what happened

Understand the specific actions or events that led to the breakdown of trust with your colleague or friend. Be open with those involved and share your feelings of upset and hurt, while allowing the other party to express their reasons, perspectives or emotions. Accept an apology when it's given and, if possible, forgive and move on. (And be prepared to give an apology and ask for forgiveness, if the boot is on the other foot.)

Ask yourself whether you are ready to trust again

After acknowledging what happened, you have to decide whether you need to or want to rebuild your relationship with the other party. This is a personal decision that no one can force you to make. It's OK if you choose not to trust them again, at least not yet – they may have hurt you so badly that you need more time to heal or you're not ready to show the vulnerability or humility required.

When you're ready, take steps to rebuild

- Trust is rebuilt over time and it's OK to take baby steps. You may even discover that the relationship will never return to the level it was before your trust was broken
- Discuss expectations and the steps required by each person to enable the relationship to be repaired.
- Establish red lines or boundaries, such as what behaviours are acceptable and what aren't. This helps create a safe space for both parties and reduces the risks of future hurt and misunderstandings.

ACCEPT THAT FEELINGS OF OVERWHELM ARE NORMAL AND MANAGEABLE

'Put in place techniques that will help you ease your burdens'

The obligations placed on us by ourselves, our work, family and friends can easily converge and overwhelm us. I'm sure you've had moments like this – the feeling of overwhelm is a very common topic among my coaching clients.

We all face moments of overwhelm no matter whether we're a busy executive, a hard-working student or a stay-at-home parent balancing children with household chores (or a combination of these!). Each of us may describe it differently, but we are referring to the same thing.

- I'm drowning in responsibilities.
- I'm always gasping for air as I race between tasks.
- I feel paralysed by the enormity of what I have to deal with.
- I've no idea where to start.
- I feel as though I'm carrying too much.

There is no simple solution to make this problem magically disappear, but I do have some practical tips and actions for you to explore. At one time or other I've successfully used each of these in my own life, as well as encouraging those I coach to try them out.

It's good to admit you're overwhelmed and to let go of things.

Know it's healthy to resolve the issue

Feeling overwhelmed is not a sign of failure but an opportunity to reassess, recalibrate and rise above the demands being placed on you. By embracing your overwhelm, you'll equip yourself with the resilience to face future challenges head-on.

Prioritize with purpose

Identify tasks that require immediate attention and those that can be deferred. You might try the well-known method of prioritizing tasks based on urgency versus importance. Your aim is to always focus your energy where it matters most and accept that you can't do everything at once.

Break down tasks into mini-tasks

It can be daunting when you're facing a large task or challenge since you may not know where to start. Try breaking the task into smaller, manageable steps and tackle these one at a time. This will make the whole process more digestible and give you a sense of accomplishment as you tick off each mini-task.

Learn from others

Seek the support and insights from those who've faced similar burdens to yours. Explore with them how you might reduce, eliminate, ignore or delay some of what is currently burdening you. You'll find that simply by talking through what is burdening you, you'll feel better.

Share the burden

When possible, ask for help by delegating tasks to others whether at work or home. Sharing the load is a quick way of lightening your burden.

KNOW THAT YOUR OWN GRASS IS GREEN

'Stop comparing yourself to others'

In today's social media age we can constantly peruse other people's lives, so it's so easy to glance across the fence and believe the grass is greener on the other side. The relentless stream of edited photos and success stories can leave us feeling inadequate, envious and questioning of our own lives. It's all too easy to forget that these glimpses don't tell the full story and that we're only getting the highlights. By constantly measuring ourselves against other people, we undermine and even ignore our own successes and achievements.

Your journey to personal fulfilment lies not in comparing yourself to the accomplishments of others but in celebrating *you* as a unique person – someone with your own milestones, challenges and triumphs. My view of life is that it's not about competition with others, but about embracing who you are and fully appreciating your achievements. It's about tending to and nurturing your own grass. As the French philosopher Voltaire famously wrote: 'We must cultivate our garden.'

The only grass that matters and needs maintaining is your own.

Celebrate your wins

Acknowledge your achievements, big and small. You could do this by writing down every day three things you're grateful for and collecting these daily lists in a gratitude journal. This practice will quickly move your focus from what you lack to the abundance that's already present in your life.

Define your success

Take time to define success in your own words. This definition should reflect what matters to you, rather than other people's standards, expectations and achievements. Display your personal definition of success somewhere you can easily see it, on your home screen or above your desk: whenever you feel envy rearing its ugly, green head, take a look at it.

Speak positively in the mirror

Develop some positive affirmations that reinforce your worth and uniqueness. Examples include saying to yourself: 'I have all I need', 'I'm content with what I'm doing and the goals I'm working towards'. By repeating these lines, you reshape your self-perception and reduce the impact and influence other people have over you.

... and speak positively to others

Recognize and celebrate the successes of those around you. This small act of giving praise creates a supportive environment, whether at home or at work, where everyone's grass can flourish side by side with yours.

KNOW WHAT SETS YOUR SOUL ON FIRE

'Identify and act on your passions'

Understanding what you're passionate about is about uncovering the core reason or purpose for your existence. It can guide your choices, influence your goals and shape who you become and the legacy you leave behind. The most successful people are those who've managed to align their life and career choices with what they are passionate about. By doing so they gain a sense of fulfilment and direction in their lives.

Identifying your passions is like uncovering a wellspring of energy that propels you towards your goals. They're typically those activities, behaviours and experiences that ignite your enthusiasm, fuel your motivation and turn your daily tasks into fulfilling achievements. In my coaching work, helping my clients discover what sets their souls on fire is instrumental to their personal growth and to creating a sense of fulfilment in their lives.

Finding your passion and purpose opens your life to amazing possibilities.

Put it into action

23

Find your passions

By practising the following tips, you'll come closer to discovering your purpose and passions.

- Identify moments that make you feel alive and fill you with enthusiasm and energy. They're often those activities where time seems to fly by because you're so immersed in the flow of what you're doing.
- Try new things that appeal to you such as attending workshops, reading different kinds of books, or engaging in as yet untried hobbies or sports.
- Identify your core values – your passions and purpose are often intertwined with what you value in life.
- Most importantly, avoid expectations imposed by family, peers or society at large – perhaps in how you spend your free time or how you choose a new career.
- Be patient with yourself – discovering what you love and are passionate about might take time to emerge.

... and pursue them

Passion without action is like a flame without oxygen – it quickly becomes extinguished. It's crucial to act on your passions, no matter how small the steps you take to start exploring them.

VALUE YOUR TIME

'Make full use of your time'

Time is the most valuable asset you possess and learning to value your time is essential because, once it's spent, it can never be reclaimed. Once you recognize this truth, you'll feel an urgency to use your time in ways that align with your deepest goals, aspirations and values.

Valuing your time goes beyond just being good at basic time management – it's a conscious decision to prioritize activities that contribute meaningfully to your life. This is a mindset shift that involves distinguishing between tasks that same seem urgent and important today, with those that align with your longer-term objectives and vision. By focusing on activities that truly matter, not only will you enhance your productivity, you will also foster a sense of fulfilment and purpose in your life.

Using your time wisely is key to a fulfilling life.

Prioritize with purpose

Understand your goals and values and always try to align your daily tasks with these overarching objectives, prioritizing your tasks in a way that reflects your needs and aspirations, both personally and professionally.

Identify time wasters

In your daily routine, identify and eliminate those tasks or situations that drain your time without significant returns. Politely but firmly decline requests that don't align with your priorities. Learning to say 'no' is liberating and it creates boundaries that leave you time to focus on tasks that truly matter.

Work smart

Try breaking down your day into focused time blocks (of, say, 30 or 60 minutes) and dedicate specific blocks to your most important tasks, without allowing any distractions. In addition, leverage tools and technology to help manage how you use your time – from task management apps to calendar reminders.

BE AN ENGAGED, ACTIVE LISTENER

'Practise listening to what others are saying – and not saying'

The art of listening to others is the foundation of meaningful interactions and relationships. Think about it – would you feel close to someone at work or in your personal life if they never seemed to listen to you?

Effective listening goes beyond the physical act of hearing words. It involves immersing yourself in the speaker's world, understanding their emotions and acknowledging their perspectives. When you deeply and intentionally listen, you are showing others that their words matter, that *they* matter, which in turn creates a space for authentic communication, respect and empathic relationships to emerge. As you become a deeper, more engaged listener, people will open up and speak more authentically, which will further deepen your relationships.

Appreciating the transformative power of listening is relatively easy; the harder part is to consistently do it well.

People will love you when they realize you deeply hear what they are communicating.

Put it into action

25

Become a deep and intentional listener

- When someone speaks to you, silence your internal chatter and let go of the urge to formulate your response while they're still talking. It's all about creating a mental space where you can absorb what they're saying to you.
- Show your commitment to listen through your non-verbal gestures, such as maintaining eye contact, nodding in agreement, or positioning your body directly towards the speaker. This kind of positive body language very powerfully conveys your presence and attentiveness.
- Be ready to summarize back to the speaker what you have heard. In doing so, don't parrot or echo (which will only irritate), but use different words. This will make them feel heard, demonstrate your active engagement and confirm your understanding of the intended message.
- Encourage the speaker to delve deeper into their thoughts and feelings by posing open-ended questions. This can deepen the conversation while showing your genuine interest.
- Never interrupt. Instead, leave the speaker to express themselves fully before responding. Interruptions disrupt the flow of communication and can signal that you don't care that much about what the other person is trying to share.
- Metaphorically step into the speaker's shoes by trying to sense and comprehend the feelings and experiences behind their words.
- Be fully present in the moment, giving your undivided focus to the speaker. This can be hard if the person speaks for a long time or if you are in a busy, distracting environment like an office. To help both of you stay present and focused, make small gestures such as giving them a nod or a smile or saying things like 'Mmm', 'Good point', 'I agree' or 'Interesting' while they're speaking to you.

STOP LIVING TO WORK

'Work to live rather than live to work'

We spend our prime adult years sacrificing personal time, health and relationships in the name of our careers and work success. It's so easy to get caught up in the whirlwind of work and find ourselves tied to the desk. Life is more than the hours we spend working, and allowing work to consume us is a path that seldom has a happy ending.

When we're older and looking back at our lives, it's highly unlikely that our work achievements and job promotions will top our list of memories. Instead, we'll be recalling moments shared with loved ones and the simple joys that made our life worth living. I doubt anyone on their deathbed will wish they had spent more time at the office or on their work laptop!

Recognizing the importance of work–life balance is the first step towards reclaiming control over your time and energy. It can also enhance your mental and physical health and your productivity. Most importantly, it ensures you'll have a more satisfying and meaningful life.

The sooner you can stop living to work, the sooner you can start truly living.

Put it into action 26

Know what's important in your life

Take a moment to think through and write down a list of all the areas of your life that are important to you. We're all unique, but typically these areas will include:

Wealth and finances	Health and exercise
Close relationships (partner, children)	Wider family
Hobbies and pastimes	Travel and Holidays
Being alone (reading, reflecting, etc.)	Learning and studying
Current work life	Career path
Volunteering and community work	Friends
Retirement	Rest and sleeping

It may be helpful to put them in a hierarchy of importance by numbering them (with 1, of course, being the most important). This will help you prioritize the areas that matter to you most.

Determine whether you need a work-life rebalance

- Ask yourself which areas are most important to your well-being and sense of fulfilment.
- Next, assess how satisfied you are in each area and reflect on the reasons why you may not feel things are in balance. This might involve you exploring why you're not making time to exercise at the gym, are overworking, not taking your paid vacation, or not finding enough time for your hobbies because your weekends are filled with family commitments.
- Start with the most important parts of your life and determine what you should (1) stop doing, (2) start doing, or (3) do differently. Turn your answers into a work – life balance to-do list.
- Work on this list on a weekly basis and have your partner or a close friend hold you to account by checking in on your progress.
- Acknowledge and celebrate your successes – such as completing a course of study, taking all of your paid vacation, or attending yoga class twice a week for three months.

KNOW THAT KARMA IS REAL

'Act positively and reap the rewards'

Life has a fascinating way of connecting our actions with their consequences. We really do reap what we sow. Think of this as our actions, words and intentions sending out ripples into the universe, shaping the course of our lives and the lives of those around us in ways we may not immediately comprehend. The energy we put out comes back to us, often when we least expect it.

- You smile and act positively all the time, so people lighten up and act positively around you.
- You seem unable to trust other people, yet are baffled why others mistrust you.
- You rarely offer to buy lunch or coffee for colleagues and then wonder why you rarely receive invites to eat with them.
- You have a habit of cheating on things like your work expenses, yet become angry when people cheat you out of money.

Life is complex and hard to fathom and we'll never know for sure how things connect, but as a minimum be ready to acknowledge the interconnectedness of all things. Prepare to embrace the potential unexpected impacts and ripple effects that your actions may have.

As a keen gardener, I like the analogy that we must be mindful of the seeds we plant around us – they may blossom as beautiful flowers or grow as annoying and invasive weeds. By consciously sowing seeds of positivity and kindness, you not only help your own future to flourish but also that of the wide world.

What goes around really does come around – beware!

Cultivate positive karma

Even if believing in karma does not come easily to you, practise the following. At a minimum you'll create a very positive environment around you.

- Strive for integrity in all your actions by letting honesty and authenticity guide your choices. Always remember that a foundation built on truths is firmer than one based on lies.
- Treat others with kindness and compassion, recognizing that every interaction is an opportunity to sow seeds of goodwill. The kindness you extend will find its way back to you in some form or other.
- Cultivate positive intentions in everything you do. When your actions are driven by a genuine desire to uplift and contribute, the world and people around will respond in kind(ness).
- Be mindful of the choices you make by pausing before reacting and consider the potential impacts of any choice open to you. As a rule of thumb, choose the path that most aligns with your values and principles.
- Let go of negative emotions and thoughts. These risk causing those around you to act negatively.
- Find time to engage in actions that contribute positively to the world around you. It can be something as trivial as picking up a piece of litter or smiling at a passer-by – all of your actions matter.

THROW AWAY YOUR MASKS

'Allow the real you to shine through'

It's time to shed those metaphorical masks we wear – those carefully constructed facades we put on to help us fit in. During my years of coaching, I have observed many different masks (I'm sure you've spotted them, too):

- Pretending to enjoy people's company, conversation or activities when you dislike them or are indifferent to them
- Acting calmly and confidently, as a way of concealing your insecurities and vulnerabilities
- Agreeing with others to avoid appearing different
- Being interested in a topic or work task even when you are feeling bored
- Pretending to be knowledgeable or sophisticated in order to fit in.

By stripping away these layers of pretence, we allow ourselves to be seen and understood for who we truly and authentically are. When was the last time others saw the real you?

Authenticity is not about showcasing perfection – it's about being real, with all your flaws and weaknesses. It takes courage and humility to reveal our vulnerabilities, but in doing so you'll find a unique kind of power – the power that comes from being unapologetically and authentically you. As you reveal your true self, you will create an environment that invites others to do the same. And the more real and authentic you allow yourself to be, the deeper the connections you will forge and the more fulfilling your life will be.

Pretending who you are might make for an easier life, but it's a life spent being false and artificial.

Put it into action 28

Be vulnerable and imperfect

Appreciate that your authenticity lies in your ability to embrace your flaws and to show your vulnerabilities – it is these that make you who you are. Embracing vulnerability starts with accepting your emotions, feelings, worries, fears and insecurities. This means acknowledging *all* your feelings, no matter whether they're sad, joyous or disturbing, and recognizing that it's OK not to feel OK.

Stop caring about what others think of you

Stop worrying about what other people say or think about you. Letting go of the fear of judgement isn't easy (and will take time), but it is such a healthy thing to do. The next time you start becoming anxious about what a colleague is saying about you or what a family member is thinking about you, recognize that what they choose to say and think is their problem, not yours. Their thoughts and comments reflect only who they are, not who you are.

Celebrate the real you

Embrace what makes you unique by celebrating your quirks, strengths and passions. Talk about the real you with other people and express your sincere appreciation to those around you who support and acknowledge the real you – the 'you' without any masks on.

KNOW WHAT YOU VALUE

'Reflect on and nurture your core values'

Our values are the fundamental qualities and principles that define who we are, shaping our decisions, actions and the life we lead. Our values are the compass that guide us through the complexities of decision-making, helping us navigate relationships, life choices and our personal growth.

Recognizing your key or core values is the first step towards aligning your life with what truly matters to you. Knowing your values enables you to make decisions that align with the real you.

Your values are those things that are important to you – the things you want, seek, need and/or enjoy in life. My values include wanting to put pen to paper, travel, be individual and grow. I wonder what yours are? Here are some of the most common values:

Achievement	Expertise	Integrity	Popularity
Authority	Fairness	Joy	Recognition
Autonomy	Faith	Justice	Reputation
Balance	Fame	Kindness	Resilience
Calmness	Firmness	Knowledge	Respect
Challenge	Friendships	Leadership	Responsibility
Community	Fun	Learning	Security
Contribution	Growth	Love	Self-respect
Creativity	Happiness	Loyalty	Service
Curiosity	Honesty	Meaningful work	Spirituality
Determination	Humour	Openness	Stability
Elegance	Influence	Optimism	Status
Ethical	Inner Harmony	Persistence	Wealth

Discovering and embracing your values is an empowering journey, steering you towards a life rich in purpose and meaning. On the next page, I'll help you discover yours.

Your values are the foundation of your life and you need to know and work with them.

Put it into action 29

Identify your values

Reflect on moments that brought you joy or frustration. What principles were at play? What annoyed you about somebody or something? What delighted you?

Your values often surface during moments of heightened emotion. For example, you may have got very upset during the Covid lockdowns that you couldn't travel overseas, so this might be a sign that travel (and experiencing other cultures) is a very important value for you. Or, your anger that a colleague is taking credit for your work may indicate that you put a high value on integrity.

Take your time to list all the possible values that resonate with you and then try to prioritize them based on which you would not wish to live without.

Work with, and not against, your core values

- Knowing your core values can help you choose your ideal job or career and avoid those that don't align. The activities, tasks and roles that resonate most with your core values are those you'll be most fulfilled and comfortable undertaking. You may value financial rewards, so a job in finance or wealth management may be best suited to your outlook, or perhaps you value service to others, so a career in social work may align well with your core being.
- When faced with important choices, always consult your core values. Whether in your career, relationships or daily routines, aligning your values with your options can help ensure you make optimal decisions.
- Your values help define your boundaries, so be ready to communicate them clearly to others to help foster understanding about who you are and what you want and don't want.
- Understanding and embracing your values is not a one-time exercise but a continual process of self-discovery and growth, too. As you evolve and gain new life experiences, recognize that your values will evolve.

STOP BLAMING OTHERS FOR YOUR MISFORTUNE

'Accept that you have control over your life'

It's very easy to feel (or pretend) that we're not in control of our lives – that we are at the mercy of events around us, such as the weather, strikes, companies going bankrupt, trains breaking down, someone dying, markets falling or partners leaving. Of course, external events impact us, but we're not simply passive bystanders – we are in charge through the choices we make and how we respond.

Take a moment to think about the incredible number of choices you make every day, even every moment. Your actions, words, gestures, decisions, thoughts, beliefs, intentions, aspirations, goals and dreams are all, at some level, *your* choices. Recognizing this truth is crucial to avoiding feeling powerless in the face of life's ups and downs and gaining a sense of control. Even your challenges and setbacks are opportunities to make (hopefully good) decisions.

Tomorrow's successes are simply a reflection of the choices and decisions you made today, so it's essential you make them well.

It's easy to blame others, but to grow you need to take ownership of your own ups and downs.

Understand your choices

To ensure you make intentional and optimal choices, be honest with yourself. This entails exploring the motives, values, biases and aspirations that guide your decisions. Don't be surprised to discover that sometimes you make choices for irrational or random reasons.

It might help if you keep a journal or diary in which you reflect on recent decisions you've made. Note down what drove you to make those choices and how comfortable you are with the outcomes of each.

View each choice as an opportunity

View each decision you need to make as a moment to grow and to learn. Having a growth mindset enables you to be an active participant in your own decision-making process and heightens your awareness that you are in control of your life.

... and own each one of them, good or bad

Owning your choices is more than just acknowledging the ones that turned out well. It's also about taking responsibility for those that proved to be wrong.

JUMP THE RED LIGHT

'Follow the rules but be prepared to break them, too'

Taking the plunge without waiting for permission can be your key to success. It's not about being reckless but rather about trusting your instincts and embracing the belief that sometimes the reward is worth the risk. It's also about acknowledging the limitations of overthinking, overplanning and waiting for multiple sign-offs. This is particularly the case when an opportunity has a short shelf-life and it's only through swift decision-making that success can happen.

This requires a mindset shift – to being willing to make bold choices by breaking the rules, venturing into uncharted territories and seeking forgiveness after the event rather than always waiting for permission beforehand.

I know from personal experience that it's hard to start making such bold decisions. I was brought up to always wait to be allowed to do something – to get down from the dining table, for example, or give my opinion in the classroom. Most people are like me and, as a consequence, are held back for fear of making mistakes, being told off or facing rejection. Part of the required mindset shift is to reframe your thinking to understand that mistakes are part of the learning process, that seeking forgiveness is a form of courage, and that we can free ourselves from always waiting and being overcautious.

> If you always wait until the light turns green, you'll miss out on so many opportunities.

Upset the apple cart

Challenge any inclination to stick to established ways of doing things just because you don't want to upset people or break the rules. Instead, try to become comfortable that not every decision requires the approval of others and that sometimes waiting for permission might result in an important opportunity being lost. Ask yourself what's the worst that could happen if you don't ask for your boss's or partner's green light.

Balance boldness with timing

Jumping the metaphorical red light doesn't mean acting with reckless abandon. It's about weighing up the risks involved, taking a thoughtful and calculated approach and understanding that timing is crucial. Each time you have an opportunity to act now, look at the pros and the cons of the situation to help manage the delicate balance between acting now or later.

Intentionally seek forgiveness

Rather than waiting to be reproached by a colleague or family member for acting so quickly or without consulting them, proactively inform them of what you've done and explain why you jumped the light.

KEEP UP TRADITIONS IN AN UNCERTAIN WORLD

'Participate in time-honoured rituals'

Our traditions and rites of passage connect us to something larger than ourselves – reflecting rich histories of cultural celebrations, seasonal rituals and pausing for life's key milestones. They provide a sense of continuity as we navigate an increasingly chaotic and uncertain world.

Pause for a moment and reflect on the festivities or rituals that fill your own calendar – Christmas, Eid, Lunar New Year, the summer solstice, Hanukkah, or Deepavali – and that's on top of the birthdays, weddings and, sadly, funerals that punctuate our year. All are moments to pause, reflect and celebrate. I encourage you to embrace them, recognizing that they ground us in something greater than ourselves and our everyday lives.

The risk is that in the busyness of our lives we dismiss them and overlook their significance, or simply rely on digital congratulations through Facebook posts or WhatsApp messages. We risk missing out on the nurturing and energizing effects of physically participating – in the laughter and joy, the dancing and singing, the food and drink consumed together, and the stories and wisdom shared.

> Our traditions provide a grounding to help us navigate the busyness and stresses of our lives.

Participate in person

Actively participate, attend and engage whenever you can, making the time to fully immerse yourself in celebratory meals, events, services and other activities. Stop making excuses that you're too busy, tired, lazy or introverted to join in.

Broaden your cultural experiences

Explore the wealth of cultural traditions beyond your own by learning about and, if possible, attending the events, rituals and celebrations of different faith traditions or cultures. As an example, my wife and I are both Christians but we had a ceremony, attended by family and friends, in a Hindu temple to mark our tenth wedding anniversary.

Create meaningful rituals

Beyond established traditions such as Christmas or Eid, why not try creating your own meaningful rituals? Whether it's a weekly family dinner, an annual retreat, or a personal reflection time, experiment with such events to help ground and energize you and those around you. It will bring your family, your friends, or your colleagues all closer together.

Involve your children

Think of yourself as a temporary torchbearer of your family and community's heritage and traditions and take time to share them with your children and other young people. For example, make putting up the Christmas tree or cooking the meal for breaking Eid a family activity. Organize an Easter egg painting workshop in your town or make Deepavali lanterns with your kids.

BE PREPARED TO BE UNPOPULAR

'Embrace authenticity over approval'

Many people gauge their value and self-worth by the number of likes and followers on social media or the signs of approval and acceptance they receive in social situations. This pursuit of universal love and acceptance can be exhausting, leading us to hold back our thoughts and feelings or make choices solely to please others. Living inauthentically for the sake of popularity is no way to live life.

The truth is, not everyone will resonate with the real you and there is immense freedom and power in accepting this fact. Acknowledging that it's OK not to be liked or loved by everyone is very cathartic. It gives you the freedom to live and express your views, values and beliefs without the constant worry of being rejected or disliked.

When you let go of the need to be universally popular and instead embrace your true self, your relationships will flourish, especially with those who appreciate you for your unique qualities. Building relationships based on authenticity can help you lead a more fulfilling life.

No longer living to please people will open you up to a more authentic life.

Watch your words and actions

Pay attention to moments in your day when you're tempted to say, agree with or do something that doesn't align with your beliefs, values or feelings. Pause in these instances and ask yourself, 'What do I really feel or think and what do I wish to express?' Summon the courage to be authentic and to resist any urge to conform. Each time you do this, you grow your inner strength and buttress your ability to be true to yourself.

Make space for meaningful relationships

Be prepared for varied reactions, especially from those who may be surprised by your refusal to conform. When you no longer say or do things merely to fit in, some friendships may fall away, but those that remain or new ones that come along will likely be more meaningful. Learn to cherish relationships with those who genuinely appreciate and value the authentic you.

FOCUS ON YOUR STRENGTHS

'You will always have weaknesses, but it's your strengths that matter'

Your success is built upon your strengths. By understanding, developing and using them well, you can propel yourself towards your goals. If you want to achieve your true potential, ensure your strengths are optimally developed and utilized.

If our strengths are so important, why, then, do we spend so much time fretting over our weaknesses? Many of us are modest and don't want to shout out about what we do well, instead being happier to talk about what we lack. What's more, we live in a feedback culture where we're encouraged to know our weaknesses and to work on eliminating them – we may, for example, take a training course to help us overcome our shyness or procrastination or hire a coach to rectify our lack of creativity or tendency to get hot under the collar. The upshot? The average person spends more time overcoming their weaknesses than they do nurturing their strengths.

This is a mistake. Yes, it's important to know which of our weaker areas may be holding us back and to be ready to eliminate them as barriers to our success. But so many of our weaknesses are simply qualities we never use or practise and that we ultimately don't need. Contrast this with our strengths – these are our habits and behaviours that we're good at doing.

Address the weaknesses that hold you back, certainly, but spend more time nurturing and practising your strengths. Maintaining your strengths is a straightforward way of elevating your performance and boosting your confidence.

Working with your strengths is so much more productive than working with your weaknesses.

Put it into action

34

Know your strengths

Think through which of your many habits, behaviours, skills and qualities define who you are and ask which of them you're really good at. Don't be shy or modest, and if needed ask other people what they see as your strengths.

To help discover your strengths, think about which qualities are behind your successes in your life. Is it your persistence, kindness, attention to detail, knowledge of French, IT skills or your presentation skills that enable you to complete your tasks well or to stand out from the crowd?

Be open about developing them

Once you've identified your strengths, give them some care and attention by deciding which of your strengths need to be honed through learning, training or intentional practice on the job.

Understand which weaknesses need attention

Acknowledge your weaknesses but don't worry about turning them all into strengths. Don't give them *any* attention unless you have weaknesses that must be overcome to ensure your personal growth and achievement of your goals. Give these specific weaknesses some attention but ignore your other weaker areas. This ensures that most of your energy is concentrated on your strengths.

BEWARE OF FREE LUNCHES

'Be on your guard for anything that seems too good to be true'

Throughout my life, I've learned a straightforward lesson: genuine freebies are scarce and even then rarely come without hidden costs or risks. Through my coaching work, I've heard so many stories of seemingly cost-free opportunities that turned out to be costly:

- You attend a free event, only to discover hidden costs such as needing to pay to stay for the entire show or even to be able to see the stage.
- You use free Wi-Fi but in doing so find that your phone data has been mined or other privacy-invading practices have occurred.
- You buy a house at a bargain price at auction, only to discover the property is in a dangerous flood zone.
- You attend a free seminar but then realize it's simply a sales pitch for a longer, paid version.
- You are offered a 'failsafe' cryptocurrency investment opportunity, only to discover that when the value falls it cannot be easily sold and all your money is lost.

When navigating our investments, relationships and personal goals, the temptation to acquire something for nothing can easily obscure our judgement and thinking. Always exercise discernment before making a decision so you can uncover any hidden costs or risks that lie beneath the surface or are lost in the fine print. Discover the costs now rather than later, when it's too late.

Pausing before accepting a free lunch can save you so much pain and grief tomorrow.

Balance enthusiasm with a bit of wise thinking

When opportunity knocks with an offer that seems a little too tempting, open your eyes wide and pause. Allow yourself the time to scrutinize, question and assess the opportunity from every angle. This considered approach will ensure your enthusiasm doesn't blind you to underlying risks or hidden complications.

Ask about the fine print

Life's free lunches often come with fine print, detailing the terms and conditions – words that we rarely read or even glance at when we sign up to something. Despite the name, they may not even be written down, so you would need to ask the right questions to learn about them. From contracts to agreements, and relationships to financial deals, understanding the fine print ensures you're fully aware of what you're getting into. You're then in a position to decide whether you walk away from your free lunch all together.

CREATE A 'TO BE' LIST

'Focus on what kind of person you want to be'

In a world filled with tasks and responsibilities, we often find ourselves caught up in a continuous cycle of 'to do' lists. While these lists can help us complete our many tasks and responsibilities and optimize what we *do*, there's an avenue of growth that also requires our attention: optimizing who we are as a person and how we wish to *be*.

Optimal 'being' is all about the habits, behaviours and traits you want to have and exhibit when working on tasks and with other people. A 'to be' list is like having a travel itinerary for your personal growth. It ensures you focus beyond your tasks, to embrace the broader picture, and reminds you to continually work on your softer, interpersonal skills. Having a 'to do' list alongside a 'to be' list helps you maintain a balanced perspective about what you need to work on.

Focusing on 'being' rather than 'doing' can help you grow and develop as a person.

Define your ideal self

Begin by envisioning your optimal self by asking what habits, behaviours, qualities and attitudes would define the best version of you. Sit quietly and allow ideas to come to you and then make a note of them.

A typical 'to be' list might include qualities such as being kind, considerate, patient, calm, thoughtful, innovative, persistent, understanding, challenging, diligent and honest. Your 'to be' list can also include your core values – after reading No. 29, you may already have a list of those.

Now consider the ways in which you might take on or improve those qualities. Be clear and descriptive in your 'to be' list – for example, if you wish to be more empathic and understanding, describe specific actions such as:

- Give more thanks and positive feedback to my spouse, partner or staff.
- In team meetings, pause before criticizing someone's idea and try to understand where they are coming from.

Refer to and update your 'to be' list

I would suggest you refer to your list, and update it, at least once a week. As with a traditional 'to do' list, the beauty of the 'to be' list lies in its adaptability – you simply add and remove tasks as they are needed or completed.

LET GO OF YOUR REGRETS

'Learn from your regrets but then put them behind you'

Ever caught yourself mulling over past decisions, replaying scenarios in your mind and wishing you could turn back time? Hindsight is a bitch – it's that constant nagging reminder of missed opportunities, wrong turns and moments you'd give anything to go back and fix. It's natural to reflect on the past, but when this reflection turns into a torrent of regrets, it becomes a mental block to your present as well as your future.

Regrets often stem from the belief that you could have navigated life differently, made better choices, or avoided pitfalls. But in your past, you didn't have the insight and wisdom you have now. It's always easy to look back and know what you would have done better. Unfortunately (or perhaps fortunately), your past will never change! So, starting now, I challenge you to stop regretting the past and instead simply learn from your regrets to help minimize future mistakes or poor outcomes ... and then let the past go.

Holding onto regrets is such a waste of your time and energy.

Put it into action

37

Extract lessons for the future

View every choice you made, good or bad, as stepping stones to your future growth. Reflect upon your mistakes by asking yourself: 'What did I learn?' How can that knowledge empower my current and future choices?

Take this newfound wisdom to set intentions for the future, asking yourself: 'What do I want to achieve and what can I do today to create a more fulfilling and successful tomorrow?'

... and then move on

Have some self-compassion by forgiving yourself for your past mistakes. Maybe you made the best decisions with the information and resources available to you at that time? Maybe you're just human?

PROCRASTINATION KILLS, SO KILL IT FIRST

'Stop delaying things until tomorrow'

So many people I coach find themselves on the edge of starting to do something, only to delay it. Sometimes their procrastination is fully justified – maybe they need to wait for further instructions and resources, finish urgent tasks first, or gain clarity on goals. And yes, sometimes you just have to wait until you're better prepared or have more time.

The danger comes when you regularly delay getting started because of some unhealthy habits:

- Perfectionism causing you to await the perfect conditions
- Fear of failure and of not doing a good job
- Being indecisive and having self-doubts
- Lack of motivation and wanting to be in the 'right' mood
- Being distracted and having poor time management
- Resisting leaving your comfort zone and taking on new things.

Making promises about tomorrow is unlikely to bring success. Instead, decide to take that important first step today.

Follow the tips on the next page to free yourself from delay and procrastination. They will help you take action and see the fruits of getting started – *now*.

If you're going to do something, do it today.

Put it into action 38

Stop the excuses

Start to appreciate that true readiness comes from actually doing something and actively engaging with your tasks. If you have a tendency to delay, waiting for perfect conditions, force yourself to start anyway – even if you spend only an hour or two today on the task.

Accept that you'll never be perfectly prepared for anything and that preparedness is a process that comes through facing tasks and challenges, learning and reflecting, and by taking decisive and corrective actions.

Have an action-oriented mindset

Yes, always give time to preparing, planning and reflecting, but as a rule of thumb have a preference for doing things. Even if you start only part of a task now, get into the habit of never leaving something for later unless you have a genuinely good reason for doing so – for example, you are waiting for needed money or a legal decision.

By regularly getting started and minimizing delay, you will slowly break free of your procrastination-related habits or mindset.

LEAVE CHILDREN TO BE THEMSELVES

'Don't be a helicopter parent'

Far too many adults are too controlling, liking things to turn out exactly as they want. This can be a fantastic skill to possess at work, but it can be disastrous when bringing up children.

Each of us, including our children, has our own personality traits, styles and characteristics, as well as unique ambitions, dreams and passions. Our role as parents is to recognize this and to bring to our parenting role a sincere willingness to allow our children to just be themselves. We should try to support them in becoming the best version of themselves, rather than wanting them to become mini-versions of us.

We all guide our children and make choices for them, often because society expects us to do so. The secret is to find a balance between guiding them and controlling their every decision. For example, you might help your child win a place to study at an excellent school, but then step back to leave them to choose optional subjects or extracurricular activities, even when their choices don't align with what you think they should choose.

Speaking as a parent of two adult children, I sometimes struggled to find this balance, but I am happy that I held back enough times so my kids could find their own paths. On the next page, I share my advice on how you can do it even better than I managed to.

The last thing a child needs is an overbearing parent trying to guide their every move.

Ask your children what they feel

Dispel the idea that your children are too inexperienced to make the right decisions, or too young to know their own feelings and thoughts. Instead, involve them in decisions about their lives. To do this well, you need to genuinely listen to them (see No. 25 for tips on how to do this). Ask them for their opinions, thoughts and suggestions and take in what they're saying. Avoid dismissing their ideas as immature or childish thinking.

Nurture healthy values

As a rule, don't force your children to do what you want, but ideally encourage them to grow some healthy and positive values and habits. This might include teaching them to say please and thank you, make their beds, be kind to their siblings and friends, and generally be polite.

The ideal is to guide them but not to micro-manage their every choice or decision. As examples:

- Encourage them to eat their vegetables, but allow them to share which vegetables they prefer.
- Motivate them to complete their homework on time, but allow them to explore how and where they like to study at home.

DON'T CUT CORNERS – IT CAN START AN AVALANCHE

'Be as diligent as you can, even when others are cutting corners'

It's so easy to find ourselves cutting corners as we rush through our lives, often in small and innocuous ways:

- Taking a one-minute shower without using shampoo or soap
- Using a dirty plate instead of washing it first
- Eating fast food, instead of cooking something healthier at home
- Not making your bed or tidying away your clothes
- Turning up late to your child's sports match rather than making an effort to be present the whole game
- Pretending you've read a report when you've only glanced at it
- Briefly parking in a restricted area rather than in a more distant car park.

These examples might only give you tummy upset or a parking ticket. But once you're habitually cutting the small corners, it's only a matter of time before you move to a different league of corner cutting that risks you being fired or arrested:

- Ignoring quality or safety checks at your factory, leading to a near-fatal accident
- Using cheaper and low-quality materials when building something
- Plagiarizing materials when writing a report or dissertation
- Cheating on your expenses or income tax reporting.

Even if you get away with your corner cutting, you'll know what you've done and by continually cutting corners you risk becoming blinded to what it means to do the right thing.

Cutting corners might save you a dollar today, but the price you'll face tomorrow might be enormous.

Put it into action 40

Think twice

Pause to think through the consequences of what you are about to do and to fully understand and take ownership of the possible consequences. Ask yourself how comfortable you are with taking the easier path compared to doing the right thing. You might be saving time, effort or money and you may feel the risk is small. But it's never about the possibility of being caught and living through the repercussions; it's the deeper question of the health of your moral values or the lack thereof. You have to become your own ethical standards officer.

Know it's a slippery path

Your actions quickly become habits and by cutting corners today, it becomes harder for you to stop cutting them tomorrow. Once you've opened the flood-gates, the water will never stop rushing through. The danger comes when your corner cutting makes you feel good and gives you a high, as you make more money, for example, or have an easier life. What's at stake, remember, are your values and worth as a human being.

DON'T CATASTROPHIZE

'Stop yourself always fearing the worst will happen'

Life is filled with uncertainties and it's natural to be cautious and to anticipate challenges. However, constantly fearing the worst, and living in a perpetual state of doom and gloom, is not only mentally exhausting, it is often unrealistic. In reality, earthquakes, both literal and metaphorical, are rare and most of our fears never materialize. The energy spent worrying about them detracts us from our ability to do things well.

It's crucial to distinguish between genuine concerns and what I'll call catastrophic thinking. While acknowledging potential pitfalls is wise, allowing unfounded fears to dominate our thoughts impedes progress and happiness.

Accepting that earthquakes, both in our personal and collective lives, are infrequent helps us redirect our focus towards constructive thoughts and actions. By breaking free from the cycle of catastrophic thinking, we can empower ourselves to confront challenges with a clear mind and to make sound decisions based on a healthy dose of realism rather than unfounded fears.

> Fearing the worst will leave you drained and anxious and in no fit state to fully embrace life.

Be systematic in assessing the risks

Unless you're a trained actuary, it isn't easy differentiating between real risks and imagined ones. Even as a layperson, though, you can identify risks by evaluating the evidence and past patterns and by trying to discern between genuine concerns that require your attention and baseless fears that can be ignored. Ask yourself, 'What evidence supports this fear? Is there a more balanced perspective?' Trying to be systematic in this way will help you challenge your negative assumptions about the future.

Change your frame of thinking

Life is uncertain and assuming the worst will only amplify your inner anxieties.

- Ground yourself in the present using mindfulness techniques. This will help you detach from catastrophic thinking and foster a clearer understanding of the current reality.
- Cultivate a mindset that embraces realism. Understand that not every challenge is a catastrophe and that setbacks are part of the journey.
- Instead of dwelling on potential problems, shift your focus to practical solutions to problems that might realistically occur. By developing a proactive approach to real challenges, you mentally focus yourself on what you can control while letting go of what you cannot (see No. 17 for this distinction).

EAT AND DRINK WELL

'Eat well if you want to flourish'

Taking a healthy approach to eating and drinking is perhaps the most important decision you'll ever make. During my coaching career, I've observed how my clients' diets have impacted not only their physical wellbeing but also their ability to perform their work. A healthy diet helps you:

- think clearly
- be creative and innovative
- remain sharp
- have stamina
- be attentive
- remain calm and composed.

Each of us is like a high-performance car: what we consume is the fuel that provides our engine with its power, efficiency and endurance. Filling yourself with poor-quality, low-nutrient food and sugar-packed drinks will make your engine sluggish and slow. Doing the opposite and consuming healthier foods and drinks will enable your engine to operate efficiently for years to come.

It isn't just a question of what you consume but also how you consume. Give your body the time to digest and process what you are putting into it. Eating and drinking in a hurry while rushing between meetings has quite a different impact compared to sitting down and slowly chewing each mouthful and calmly sipping a drink.

By adopting mindful eating and drinking habits today, you help ensure the rest of your life will be as long, healthy and fulfilling as possible.

We become what we consume, and thankfully we can control what we consume.

Consume intelligently

These are the healthy eating and drinking rules that I have learned to follow:

- Drink plenty of clean water throughout the day. Our bodies are 70 per cent water and it only stands to reason that we need to keep it replenished with its main component. Try having a large water container by your side while working; it will visually remind you to take regular sips.
- On a weekly basis, ensure that you consume a well-balanced combination of fruits, vegetables, whole grains and lean proteins.
- Minimize eating processed products. Instead, cook your own dishes using basic ingredients such as rice, raw vegetables, pulses, and pieces of fish or meat, depending on your dietary preferences.
- Make time to eat mindfully and to slowly chew and enjoy your food. Leave your TV and smartphone switched off and talk to your dining companion(s) instead!
- Be conscious of the size of your meal portions and minimize snacking between meals.
- If suitable, fast to give your body a rest from having to continually digest food. You might create a rule that, once or twice a week, you eat only one light main meal.

SEE THE FOREST, NOT THE TREES

'Take in the bigger picture'

In our busy lives, it's so easy to become caught up in the details and small issues – tasks that need completing, requests responded to and issues addressed. Using the time-honoured forest metaphor, these are the individual trees and straggly undergrowth that always seem to need our attention. Most of the time it's OK to attend to the detail, but sometimes it can be helpful to step back to take in the bigger picture of your life or career and to explore how the nitty-gritty things you are focusing on are connected to the bigger issues. How is that forest growing? Is it flourishing?

Stepping back to see the whole forest can help give purpose and meaning to your tasks and challenges and ensure that where you're spending your time and energy is aligned with your overall plans and direction. In this way, you're more likely to discover patterns and synergies between the everyday things you're focusing on, enabling you to plan ahead and find the best path through all those trees.

Pausing to step back and see the bigger picture might give you the answers you need.

Take time to step back

Regularly take a pause to assess your priorities and to explore how well your tasks (the trees) are aligned with your overall goals and aims (the forest). You might do this on a daily or weekly basis and it is a good activity to do while reviewing and updating your 'to do' list: by stepping back you can ensure that your list is aligned with your overall priorities and direction (and remember that 'to be' list in No. 36!).

Delegate or automate the details

Whenever you're able to delegate or to automate some of your smaller tasks, you're giving yourself time and energy for things that really matter. At the risk of labouring that forest analogy a bit too much, when some of your trees can be managed more efficiently by technology or other people, you're better able to focus on the broader landscape.

TOGETHER FOREVER TAKES INVESTMENT

'A lifelong relationship will test you, but it's worth it'

Committing to a life together might be one of the greatest decisions you ever make, but may easily be your most challenging to live with. Any relationship can be hard to maintain and grow, so it's totally understandable that the thought of living together and committing to being with one person can seem daunting and even scary.

After 25 years of married life, I know that being and staying together is no walk in the proverbial park. Both partners will face misunderstandings, emotional clashes, differences of opinion, and competing ambitions and needs. Overcoming these challenges requires both sides to develop skills such as compromise, negotiating, empathy, compassion, forbearance and forgiveness. For many, the learning curve is too steep and as a result so many marriages and relationships break down.

Perhaps you're now asking: is it really worth it? Yes, of course it is! Committing to live together is an opportunity for two people's energies, dreams, hopes and ambitions to intertwine and to create something deep and meaningful. While choosing to be single is just as valid, of course – with its own joys and difficulties – with patience and effort any long-term relationship can become a journey of insights, experiences, growth and learnings. And through appreciating the positive moments and navigating the more difficult times, both partners can develop their capacity for wisdom, love and understanding of life.

Committing to another person can be both the most fulfilling and challenging decision you'll ever make.

Put it into action 44

Never lose your individuality

Allow your partnership to become a balance of, on the one hand, coming together to create shared experiences and life goals such as buying a house or having children and, on the other, making space for each partner's personal needs and aspirations. These might include having your own exercise regime, studying for a course, spending time with your own friends or even travelling alone.

Empathy and communication are key

Try to see things through your partner's eyes. You may not always agree with their opinions, desires, needs or actions, but have enough patience and empathy to try to understand why they think and feel the way they do. Developing this understanding involves being open and honest in your conversations, freely expressing your feelings, hopes, worries and fears, and encouraging your partner to do the same. For me, this is true compassion and love and is the foundation for any long-term relationship.

Embrace change and challenges together

Arguments and misunderstandings tend to arise when you both face changes or challenges, such as dealing with illness, losing a job and income, moving home, or – God forbid – losing a child. Given we are all constantly subject to change, it's crucial that both of you help each other to recognize and navigate whatever difficulties those changes may bring (see No. 17 on resilience). It is at these moments that the communication and mutual understanding so carefully built up through the months and years pay dividends, helping you weather the storms as a pair rather than allowing the difficulties to pull you apart.

Staying single might be right for you

Not everyone chooses to enter a long-term relationship and staying single offers freedom and the opportunity to focus on your passions and goals without compromise. While it may lack the shared experiences of a partnership, staying alone can bring its own profound sense of accomplishment and contentment.

DON'T BE A PERFECTIONIST

'Don't obsess about getting everything right'

Getting things perfect can seem like the easy path to success. However, my experiences and observations as a coach have taught me that doing things perfectly isn't the answer to a successful life. Instead, perfectionism is often a hindrance: it can slow down your progress and leave you so obsessed with getting everything right that you miss the bigger picture and the joy that comes with the journey.

Being a perfectionist often comes with an obsessive and competitive mindset that sets unattainable standards and goals and leaves you fearing making mistakes, coming second or even getting started at all. This isn't a healthy way to spend your time and it'll have a significant cost on your quality of life, leading to low energy, poor health and burnout.

Being successful doesn't equate with being flawless, but instead comes from being thorough, consistent and timely. Yes, sometimes you need to perfectly dot every 'i' and cross every 't', but at other times different criteria determine what your success needs to look and feel like.

Dotting all of your 'i's and crossing all your 't's can be a very unproductive use of your time.

Celebrate progress and efficiency over coming first

The secret is to strive to complete tasks well without succumbing to the all-consuming pressure of achieving perfect outcomes. This involves allowing yourself to want to do things well but without being obsessed with finishing first or being the person whose work is flawless. This can be a hard habit to change, particularly if you're a first-born child whose parents pushed you to constantly come out on top in every test, exam or game.

Part of letting go of perfectionism is learning to appreciate the journey rather than being preoccupied with winning the race. Try to be happy with having done the best job you could, rather than with your presentation getting more applause than your colleagues' or your essay getting the highest mark in your cohort. This relates back to the idea about not comparing yourself with others we looked at in No 22.

If you're still not convinced of the need to change your thinking, then do it for your health. Understand that if left unchecked, the relentless pursuit of perfection will take an unhealthy toll on your mental and emotional health. Then, one day, you'll become too ill to achieve perfection anyway.

LEARN UNTIL YOUR DYING BREATH

'Develop and hold on to a learning strategy'

In today's fast-changing world, the key to being valuable and relevant is to continually learn new things. This often involves letting go of what you have previously learned and learning things afresh. As well as being essential to remaining capable and employable, this constant learning can leave you feeling more empowered, positive, confident and motivated to take on any new challenges and opportunities that come your way.

Everywhere we look, we see people needing to learn and study things. Refusing to constantly learn is no longer an option, no matter who or where you are in life:

- Lawyers must remain up to date on new legislation and legal developments.
- Teachers have to study and attend training to remain on top of changing ways of learning and subject content.
- Retirees need to navigate new technologies to access online services and goods.
- Sportspeople must continually refine the way they compete in their events.
- Leaders have to continually explore new leadership concepts and tools.

Today, learning isn't confined to classrooms or structured courses. Instead, it's available everywhere and in so many forms, making it a lifelong and dynamic process.

Spend your entire life learning, unlearning and relearning.

Become a positive and continuous learner

- Adopt a positive learning mindset where you treat learning not as a chore but as an adventure. When you feel that what you're studying or learning is dull or tedious, ask yourself whether you need to master and understand that particular topic or subject. It's so much easier to absorb new ideas and information when the learning is satisfying and enjoyable.
- Be ready to let go of any lazy learning habits and to unlearn any out-moded knowledge and information. Make room for up-to-date concepts and thinking.
- Don't just focus on learning what you need to remain up to date in your current job. Broaden your learning by being open, curious and inquisitive about anything and everything around you – in your industry and beyond.
- Explore all the ways of learning available to you – from online courses, to using ChatGPT and other AI-driven tools, to learning on the job, through to seeking out a mentor, study group, events or podcasts.
- It's a great idea to keep a summary of your learning so you can refer back to it from time to time. This will reinforce the new insights, lessons learned and discoveries you've acquired.

STAND TALL

'Pay attention to your body language'

Appreciating the significance of your body language as a silent communicator is essential. Your non-verbal cues and signals shape how others view you and how well they like, listen and agree with you.

Consider when and how your body language has exuded positivity, confidence and openness. You may have noticed how this created an open, collaborative and inviting atmosphere in your relationships, business or otherwise. By contrast, ask yourself what kinds of body language – perhaps in yourself or that you've witnessed in others – might have seemed depressed, negative or uptight, impeding the chances of a successful interaction.

As well as influencing others, your body language affects your self-perception and mindset. This is because of the connection between our minds and our bodies. For example, the mere act of physically standing upright and carrying yourself with confidence will positively impact your state of mind and self-confidence.

Our non-verbal communication is so important and thankfully is easy to master.

Put it into action

47

Become observant of yourself

There are many tips for optimizing your body language. Here are some that my coaching clients find particularly useful:

- Maintain eye contact with people to help convey interest and sincerity. Too many people avert their gaze, which can be very off-putting.
- Ensure your facial expressions align with the messages you are trying to convey. Unless you intentionally wish to be stern or angry, be sure to smile as often as possible.
- Use hand gestures to help you come across as warm and approachable and appear less stiff or robotic.
- Project confidence with a firm handshake and by maintaining an upright posture when standing or sitting.
- To create a deeper connection with someone, copy their body movements – if they cross their legs, sit back or start smiling, subtly mirror what they are doing. Don't overdo this, however, as it will begin to grate.
- Recognize and adapt your body language depending on the specific context, including the cultural background of those you're with.
- Finally, give time to how you look. Make sure that your clothes, grooming and hygiene – your whole appearance – align with how you wish to be viewed or perceived.

NEVER SETTLE

'Don't be content with a second-best life'

Life is an extraordinary opportunity for each of us to follow our dreams, passions and talents and settling for anything less risks leaving us missing out on the full range of experiences that our lives have to offer.

Life is too short to stay in jobs that are only OK, relationships that are just lukewarm, or places that don't excite you. Staying with people or in careers that are only 'good enough' or are 'all right' might feel comfortable and safe, but is it what your future self would want you to do? Is it what you, now, really want to do?

It's very common for people not to reach their full potential and it's often because we don't know any better or because we fear the unknown or failure. Even with encouragement and support, not everyone will take the plunge – they'll never know what boundaries could have been pushed and what untapped potential and experiences might have awaited them. Don't be like them and lose the opportunity to live an extraordinary life, one that's aligned with your dreams, passions and potential.

If you want an 'ok life' then settle, but if you truly want to live then stop and think before settling.

Put it into action

48

Keep your dreams centre stage

Never lose sight of your aspirations, dreams and life goals – think, write and talk about them. These are not simply directions to the next town, they're what determine the direction of the rest of your life. Visualize what achieving them looks and feels like – try drawing pictures of that moment, whether that's inside your head or on paper. I want you to be so determined to chase your dreams that you'll never be able to settle for anything less.

Expect uncomfortable changes and choices

Learn to expect constant changes in your life as you chase your dreams and aspirations – after all, the only people immune to change are those who've settled for their less-than-fulfilling current life. Similarly, be ready to need to make courageous and risky-looking choices – choices that push you out of your comfort zone.

FILL YOUR PIGGY BANK

'Budget so you can save money and build investments'

Saving money can have a profound impact on your life. As well as improving your bank balance, it gives you more freedom to pursue your dreams and create the life you want. Nothing can hamper aspirations as much as lack of money. Building up your wealth will allow you to act with more confidence about what you're able to do and achieve and to have less fear about what can go wrong.

By exercising discipline in managing your money, you'll be able to gain control over your financial situation, reducing any money-related anxiety and worries. Managing your finances well extends beyond simply saving some of your monthly salary – it encompasses skills such as mindful spending, budgeting and setting achievable financial goals.

Regularly saving can help you achieve future financial independence.

Put it into action

49

Practise these six financial habits

1. Make saving a mandatory part of your monthly routine. To avoid the temptation of skipping a month, set up an automatic transfer of a fixed percentage of your salary to a savings or investment account.
2. Use a budgeting app on your phone or a simple spreadsheet on your laptop to itemize your income, expenses and savings. Review and adjust your budget regularly or as needed.
3. As your savings build up, explore investment options that give you a better return than simply earning bank interest. Seek professional advice if needed.
4. Make a plan to manage and pay off any existing debts, starting with those with the highest interest and fees.
5. Become very intentional about what you spend your money on and try to avoid impulse buys. Keep an eye out for vouchers, discounts and special offers on things you wish to purchase.
6. Learn about financial matters to ensure you're up to date about tax changes, investment options and other relevant financial topics.

CELEBRATE GROWING OLDER

'Face ageing with positivity and hope'

In a world that seems to glorify being young, it's easy to view growing old as something best avoided or at least ignored. When we think of ageing, our first thoughts are usually of bodies in decline – with issues such as hip replacements, dementia and arthritis coming to mind. While we will inevitably face more health issues as we grow older, and no matter when you think old age starts, our later years can bring some amazing positives:

- Our life experiences give us wisdom to appreciate what's important and what we value – including in our relationships, experiences and ways of being.
- We are more likely to appreciate what we have and to be satisfied and at peace. We may no longer yearn for material things or hanker so much after accolades and recognition, even if we continue to achieve.
- If we retire or begin to work less, we have more time and insight to help others and give back – perhaps by guiding the younger generations or by doing voluntary work.

By embracing these positives, we can shift our mindset to view the later chapters of our lives with renewed enthusiasm and fulfilment – to seek out and appreciate the positives that accompany the passage of time.

You can either fight getting older or embrace it – the latter choice is so much easier and more fulfilling.

Put it into action

Feel good about ageing

Take stock of your accomplishments and celebrate them, nurturing a sense of gratitude for what you've experienced and who you've become. Embrace the opportunity to discover new things that help keep you energized and let go of the things that bring little value. Seek out meaningful growth, experiences and connections – it might be new skills, hobbies or travel.

Prioritize well-being

No one can grow old and ignore their health – you might want to, but issues will come knocking. Be proactive and follow a plan that focuses on maintaining your physical, mental and emotional health. Combine regular physical exercise with mental exercise, a balanced diet and mindful activities such as yoga, walking in nature, intentional breathing and meditation.

Connect with others

Invest time in nurturing relationships that really matter to you and let go those that don't. If you're tempted to spend most of your older years alone, remember that sharing experiences and moments with others is a fundamental part of being human.

And finally, recognize the value of your life's lessons and the wisdom you've gained by giving your time to help and mentor others.

LET OTHER PEOPLE BE YOUR MIRROR

'Learn from the people around you'

Everybody we encounter is a mirror reflecting elements of ourselves, offering us opportunities to deepen our self-awareness and accelerate our personal development.

We tend to see ourselves in others, even if unconsciously. For example, when you spot a weakness in another person, it's probable that you're observing a fault that you also possess. Likewise we might also see and admire in others what we ourselves lack – a positive quality such as being organized or patient, or a skill we'd like to acquire.

Observing others can even reveal qualities that we've never thought of before – highlighting poor characteristics that you'd never wish to emulate or positive ones you'd love to master.

It's not enough to recognize ourselves in others, we must also be willing to act on that recognition – learning from and evolving based on what we have observed. As I write this, I'm reminded of the numerous mirrors that have graced my own life, from bosses and colleagues to family and friends – people who've helped me better understand myself and nurture my strengths.

Seeing yourself in other people can help you to become self-aware and grow.

Seek your reflection without judgement

Actively learn from the people around you, seeking to observe the patterns in your own behaviours that you need to recognize and work on. When you see weakness in others, resist the urge to criticize or judge; instead, ask yourself whether you're guilty of the same poor habit or behaviour.

Close relationships are your main mirrors

Those close to you are the most powerful mirrors you'll ever have and are a fantastic opportunity for you to learn. However, since they're close to you, it's likely that their weaknesses will really annoy you, while their positive qualities may overwhelm you or make you feel jealous. Work through these feelings and give these people positive feedback when you observe them doing something well, while resisting the urge to critically lecture them when they appear to do something that annoys you.

Seek diverse mirrors

Surround yourself with a diversity of people in terms of age, gender, class, race, ability or sexuality, among other things. They'll be sure to offer you a wealth of divergent perspectives, experiences and expertise. This diversity will provide you with a broader range of insights than if you simply remain around people like yourself.

FIND YOUR HIGHER MEANING

'Seek out your own source of meaning'

At some point in our lives we wonder about the meaning of it all. This often arises when someone close to us dies or falls seriously ill, when we go through a divorce, or face some other difficult change. In these moments, some are able turn to deeply held religious beliefs while others struggle to know where to turn for comfort and answers.

Discovering your own source of meaning and higher beliefs is important for your well-being, particularly in your darkest moments when you may otherwise feel totally lost. By having your own source of meaning, you are able to:

- live and express yourself more authentically with a sense of purpose and meaning
- fall back on your beliefs during challenging moments, when prayers, meditations or other rituals can provide much-needed comfort and strength
- more easily step back from events and situations and see them as part of a bigger picture.

Searching for our own source of meaning recognizes that each of us is unique, and what brings some people compassion, strength and understanding may to others feel empty and hollow. While some find solace in a formal religion, others simply need to meditate outside in nature. The danger comes when you adopt the practices of your parents or friends without ever asking yourself whether their beliefs and practices resonate with what you feel and need.

> Finding some higher meaning can help ground you and put your everyday challenges into perspective.

Put it into action

52

It's OK to change

We all evolve as we grow older and it's understandable if the beliefs instilled in you during childhood no longer seem to resonate with you today. It may feel disloyal to your parents if you explore other paths and beliefs, but maybe you need to as part of your own journey. After all, there's little point in holding on to beliefs that offer little meaning to you, nor bring any comfort or support in your difficult times.

Take a deep look

If you're lacking beliefs or your current ones no longer serve you, make time to discover others that may resonate with you. Explore what's out there by attending spiritual and religious events, reading sacred works, or listening online to religious teachers. It's possible, of course, that nothing will resonate and that you discover that your ultimate faith is in humanity.

Adopt a pick-and-mix approach

If you struggle to find one form of spirituality and higher meaning that feels right for you, it's OK to dip into a variety of rituals or practices that hold meaning for you. Perhaps spend time sitting in your local church, temple or mosque, giving thanks to a higher power; practise a daily meditation in a quiet place in your home or garden; or make time to be alone in nature – woodlands are, I find, especially consoling places.

BEFRIEND YOUR DEMONS

'Deal with your dark side – those things you keep hidden'

It's important to acknowledge and embrace the darker aspects of our nature – those desires, habits and behaviours that remain hidden away and unspoken. Perhaps we harbour deep feelings of envy, anger or bitterness, or have violent or sexual feelings that make us feel guilty or ashamed.

We cannot hope to grow and be truly successful if we never confront these uncomfortable sides of our personality. Some people spend years hiding from them, even going so far as to deny they exist.

Yet all the while the buried darkness is affecting their lives in all kinds of unhealthy ways.

Through my years of coaching people, I understand how scary and uncomfortable it can be to simply admit your demons exist, let alone deal with them. Yet it's crucial to understand and accept these aspects of yourself and to stop seeing them as your enemy. Instead, embrace them as part of who you are. If necessary, reach out to others – whether a friend, counsellor or therapist – to help you come to terms with whatever is brooding inside you. By doing so, you'll open the door to profound personal growth.

Befriend and work with your demons, otherwise they'll control you.

Put it into action

53

Own your demons

It's not easy but I encourage you to be very honest with yourself by naming and acknowledging your demons. Without doing this, it's virtually impossible to be able to work through them. You don't have to condone your embarrassing or hidden desires, behaviours or habits, but simply name them to yourself.

Open up to somebody

You could stay silent and try to work on them by yourself but you'll struggle. Our demons are nearly always addictions of some kind and you'll recall from No. 18 that opening up to others is a key part of overcoming any addiction. With very embarrassing or taboo issues you may be understandably hesitant to share them with anybody – not even with a professional, let alone your partner, family member or friend.

Overcome your worries about feeling embarrassed or being judged by others and find a professional therapist – someone whom you can open up to and who will guide and support you along the journey of dealing with your darker side. They've heard it all before, so nothing is going to surprise or shock them.

STOP WAITING TO BE HAPPY

'Stop saying 'I'll be happy when . . .'

In our pursuit of a successful life, many of us make the mistake of linking our happiness and success to future events and achievements. We tell ourselves we'll be happy when ...

- I finish my degree
- I win a promotion
- I'm married
- I retire
- I move home
- I sell my company
- I switch career
- I find a new partner
- I emigrate
- I'm fit and healthy

In my coaching, I meet many people who are postponing contentment, happiness and success to a distant point in the future. Many are enduring unhappiness today in the hope that things will turn around tomorrow. This is a delusion. Happiness is not a destination but a state of being, and the pursuit of a better tomorrow shouldn't come at the expense of feeling content today.

By recognizing that happiness is all in the journey, you release yourself from the pressure of needing to attain some far-off goals in order to feel happy and content. You can then learn to see happiness in each experience met, connection made and learning undertaken. Once you begin doing this, you unlock your potential to experience joy and contentment every day.

Happiness is a choice you make each day, not something to wait to experience in the future.

Put it into action 54

Change your approach

Think through your patterns of thought and behaviour and ask yourself to what degree you have the 'I'll be happy when ...' tendency. You may not be able to stop thinking this way overnight, but don't allow such thoughts to make you unhappy with your present circumstances.

- If you feel you'll be happier in a larger home with a garden, be careful not to become upset and overcritical about your current small apartment.
- When you sense you'll only be happy when you have a child, don't be depressed and upset with each passing day that you remain childless.
- If you believe that you'll only be finally content when your divorce comes through, don't make every remaining day of being married brim with bitterness and anger.

Be happy today

Rather than spending today longing for potential future achievements, start feeling gratitude for your life today, *as it is now*. This could be appreciating how lucky you are to have your cosy, small apartment or valuing the freedom you currently have as a couple without any childrearing responsibilities.

This advice may sound 'easier said than done' but it reflects a truth that we're all on a journey and we owe it to ourselves to make the most of each passing day.

SAY SORRY

'Have the courage to admit when you're wrong'

The ability to express regret, acknowledge mistakes and admit you're wrong is invaluable. Sadly, too many people have too much pride and ego to recognize this and view apologetic behaviour as weakness. This can cause no end of trouble in relationships of every kind, personal and professional: no one likes or trusts a person who refuses to recognize when they're wrong and never demonstrates any humility.

Showing remorse and acknowledging when your words and actions are wrong are skills that can be learned and mastered through practice. By doing so, you diminish the power of your ego and pride and strengthen your humility and emotional intelligence. You'll feel better and your relationships will become more trusting, open and collaborative.

Saying 'I'm sorry' can have a profoundly positive impact in your life and relationships.

Put it into action

55

Apologize in the moment

Get in the habit of apologizing as soon as you realize it's the right thing to do, rather than prevaricating and delaying. Saying sorry now reduces any resentment and upset that might otherwise build up. Sometimes you may need to follow up on your initial 'in the moment' apology, because at that time the other party may have been too upset or emotional to hear you clearly.

Be sincere

A genuine apology is always about more than words (in your email, message or conversation). Your sincerity should also be visible in your body language and, most importantly, in your follow-up actions. Be ready to act in ways that demonstrate that you've learned from your mistake, that you won't repeat it and that you value the relationship with those you upset.

Learn from your actions

Understand the root cause of your actions and treat the need to apologize as an opportunity to self-reflect and to approach things more carefully next time.

Accept the apologies of others

When the roles are reversed and other people apologize to you, be prepared to accept what they say and try to let go of any upset or grudges you may be holding on to.

ACCEPT THAT FATE WILL THROW YOU A CURVEBALL

'Deal with life's unfairness'

Just when you think everything's great and you've got it all figured out, life has a nasty habit of throwing curveballs in your direction. It's never a question of *if*, but a matter of *when*. Sometimes it can be as dramatic as your partner walking out, having a miscarriage, or a sudden job loss, but often it can be something more ordinary, less life-changing, such as a missing out on your first choice of university. It reminds me of the old Woody Allen joke: 'If you want to make God laugh, tell him your plans.'

These moments often leave us shocked and disoriented and it's only natural that we ask, 'Why's this happening to me?' or 'What have I done to deserve this?' From there, it's so easy to play the victim card and to become bitter and cynical.

But as painful as it is, an unexpected and unpleasant event might just be the wake-up call your life needs. Treat such moments as opportunities to re-evaluate and realign your life, to re-examine your choices and decide whether you need to alter the course of your life's journey.

Accepting that life can be unfair, and learning to live with this reality, is very healthy and liberating.

Put it into action

56

Don't automatically take it personally

Whenever you've been impacted by bad news, it's helpful to understand what's happened and to ask what you could have done differently. What did you miss? Was it your fault? Sometimes there's an easy answer: you didn't study enough, you missed signs that your company was struggling, that your job performance was weak, that your partner was very unhappy.

But often there's no simple explanation. There's no way you could have known or even avoided what happened. We justifiably call these events 'fate', 'acts of God' or plain old-fashioned bad luck. If this is the case, don't waste your energy blaming yourself – simply tell yourself that you've been unlucky and that you'll get through this.

View life's curveballs as catalysts for positive change

When fate has destroyed your plans by taking away something you were hoping for – a college place, marriage, job security or your full health – don't fall into despair and give up on that goal, dream or ambition. Instead, view this as an opportunity to reflect and to ask what you truly want and what would be an alternative and fulfilling outcome. Take some time to explore the available options and opportunities that remain open to you.

DON'T JUMP INTO EVERY CONFLICT

'Pick your battles wisely'

It's very tempting to jump into every conflict and disagreement that comes your way – everything from opportunities to point out that someone is wrong through to standing up to someone's unacceptable behaviour. Too many of us, though, jump in for the wrong reasons – driven by our emotions, ego and a sense of hurt rather than by principles and fact. What's more, if you're the type who always wants to right wrongs and challenge people, then you're probably heading into battle every single day of your life.

Every fight leaves a mark and engaging in conflicts can easily strain relationships, heighten tensions and damage your and others' well-being. The sensible course of action is to pick your battles wisely. Understand the nuances at play and decide which misunderstandings, injustices and disagreements really need your attention and involvement. Otherwise, show restraint by walking away. By doing so you'll help preserve relationships and everyone's well-being.

Wisely choosing when you avoid or become involved in conflicts is an important life skill.

Put it into action 57

Know what is driving you

Before entering any fight, ask yourself what's driving you to get involved. Is it your ego and emotions? Or is it a cool, objective decision that had led you to this course of action? If in doubt, pause and take a breath – be sure you're not simply entering a conflict for the sake of your pride and a desire to have the last word (on that, revisit No. 16).

Think through your principles and values. These will help you determine the kinds of issues that are worth your intervention. Perhaps you value kindness and fairness, so seeing your colleague being bullied is a definite red line. Knowing your values makes it much easier for you to decide whether a brewing conflict really deserves your time and energy.

Choose the battleground

If you're sure you need to intervene, then make sure you choose the appropriate battleground. Which situations are best handled privately in one-on-one conversations and which can be handled in group or team settings? Similarly, think through whether it's appropriate to conduct any potentially tense discussions by email or on the phone or whether they need to happen in person.

Learn to do nothing

The most difficult skill, particularly if you're naturally hot-headed or are a fighter, is to know when to show restraint and do nothing. Not involving yourself and appearing to let others win can be seen as a sign of weakness, when in truth it's actually a sign of maturity and self-control. You can develop these qualities by simply making yourself step back from every conflict you do not need to be part of. By doing this a few times, it'll become easier and you'll find that your ego and emotions will have less of a hold over you.

OVERCOME YOUR KRYPTONITE

'Know what paralyses you'

We all have elements in our lives that can render us powerless and hold us back from our full potential. Just as Superman became paralysed when in contact with the shiny green rock from his home planet, you too may have vulnerabilities that weaken or even paralyse you.

Discovering what is your own version of kryptonite will involve having an honest exploration of your triggers and fears, as well as knowing which situations to avoid that have the potential to derail you. Our kryptonite typically comes in two forms:

- In someone's presence you find yourself unable to freely express yourself. It might be an overbearing parent or sibling with whom you have too much history and tension, or an overcritical and opinionated colleague or friend who shoots down anything you say.
- Faced with a particular task – maybe a presentation or an interview – we find ourselves paralysed with fear and struggle to move forward; we may be literally lost for words.

To live to your full potential, it's time you discover what your kryptonite is and learn how to overcome its paralysing effects.

Finding ways of dealing with people or events that paralyse you is essential to your life's success.

Identify the kryptonite

Spend time listing your past experiences that left you feeling weakened and unable to operate at 100 per cent. Your kryptonite list will probably fall into two different buckets, as we've seen:

1. People in whose presence you struggle to be yourself.
2. Tasks and activities that leave you immobilized.

Develop coping strategies

Create some boundaries and rules to protect you from people and situations that trigger and paralyse you. This might involve deciding not to connect with particular people, or at least to minimize your interactions. When you can't avoid them, you should develop workarounds to help you cope. For example, if you find it hard to speak up and express your feelings when in someone's presence, share your opinions or comments in writing instead.

Similarly with any tasks and activities that cause you to become paralysed, experiment with solutions like delegating and outsourcing them or changing the form of the task – such as pre-recording a message rather than speaking live and in person.

You may also need to push yourself to learn new skills or seek professional help to overcome your paralysing reactions to a person or a task. For example, you could take a training course in being assertive or find a public speaking coach.

Finally, be willing to share your vulnerabilities with family, close friends and colleagues – people who'll give you moral support and encouragement, and even some helpful tips.

KEEP YOUR MIND HEALTHY

'Don't keep quiet about your mental health'

Our mind is the machine through which we live – through it we experience reality and create our perceptions, choices and responses to the world around us. When our minds are healthy, we're able to feel positive and see things clearly, take sound decisions and live a fulfilling life.

Maintaining our mental health isn't easy given the range of pressures and challenges we face – from personal challenges and peer pressures through to our relationship, work and financial worries. For many, simply getting through each day can feel like a big mental achievement. I see this in my coaching work, where clients are trying to optimally function while facing all kinds of mental struggles that are impacting them in so many different ways – as migraines, stress, inability to concentrate or relax, burnout, insomnia, worry overthinking, panic attacks, irritability and depression.

Being mentally healthy is more than simply being free of any recognizable mental illnesses. It's about not being plagued by overwhelming anxieties worries or negative feelings and instead being able to function in a calm and balanced way.

> Your mental health is just as important to maintain as your physical health.

Put it into action

59

Speak up

Overcome any tendency to keep quiet about your mental health for fear of being seen as weak and unable to cope. We're not helped by the continuing stigma associated with having any kind of mental illness and by the fact that others cannot easily tell when you're not 100 per cent mentally fit. For these reasons, the onus lies with you to speak up and share what you're experiencing to enable others to understand and help. You never know: you speaking out may well help them with *their* mental health.

Be wary of superficial advice

Don't allow other people to give you their advice and opinions if they don't truly appreciate what you're going through. Most people downplay what others face by making well-meaning but harmful comments such as 'You'll feel better after a good night's sleep', 'Get a grip – you'll be fine', or, worse, 'Be a man [*sic*] and get a hold of yourself ...'.

Recognize it's an ongoing journey

Seek good treatment and help for your immediate issue – be it anxiety, panic attacks or insomnia – but don't stop there. Instead, view your current mental challenge as a wake-up call to take care of your overall mental health through adopting some healthy mental habits and behaviours. These might include:

- stress-reduction techniques
- mindfulness
- walking away from toxic people
- overcoming your addictions
- talking kindly to yourself
- facing your fears and dark side.

Many of these are covered in this book. The key is to experiment to find out which specific healthy habits and behaviours help you and then to make them a part of your daily and weekly routines.

SEEK DEEP FRIENDSHIPS

'Value quality over quantity when it comes to friendship'

Stop being concerned about how many followers you have on social media or how many friends invite you down to the pub or out to dinner. True success isn't about the number of friends you have; what's key is the depth and authenticity of those connections.

The ideal is to have some treasured deep friendships that stand the test of time – with people who are there for you in the bad times as well as the good and who provide a sense of belonging that supports your mental and emotional well-being. These are the people who accept you for who you really are and act as pillars of strength when needed.

Such friendships are rarely quickly established but instead require time wisdom and energy if they are to mature and endure. They deepen through shared experiences, open, honest and mutual communication, and a genuine willingness to support each other's journeys.

It's far better to have a small number of meaningful friendships rather than dozens of superficial friends.

Choose your friendships very carefully.

Put it into action

60

Seek genuine connections

Take a look at your range of friendships today and list those friends with whom you feel a deep and meaningful connection – it is these relationships that you should invest in and treasure. Your other friendships may feel important too, but when choosing where to give your time and attention, your focus should be on your deeper friendships.

When meeting new people, be discerning and invest your energy only in relationships with those you feel will become meaningful friends.

Maintain your friendships

Maintaining a good friendship requires that both parties make an effort – by investing their time, attention, trust and openness.

It's a two-way process of give and take – sometimes you are the shoulder to cry on and at other times your friend is there when you are facing a struggle. Be kind and forgiving with close friends – occasionally you may need to apologize for neglecting them and another day they might be saying sorry for doing something that upset you.

TAKE BABY STEPS BEFORE YOU RUN

'Practise patience'

Patience is an important virtue in all parts of life – whether it's mastering a skill, developing a new habit, achieving a personal goal or simply dealing with what life throws at you. Your ability to be patient might be the biggest key to your success, since having a little patience can help you in so many ways. It can help to:

- avoid moving too quickly and running out of steam or hitting an obstacle unprepared
- wait for the right moments while remaining committed to objectives
- pause to review and readjust how you'll work towards your goals
- sustain momentum in the face of setbacks and challenges.

In our earliest years, we learn to walk by patiently taking baby steps – standing up, wobbling as we take a step or two, before falling down and trying again. As adults, too, in many of the tasks we face, success is possible only if we deliberately take baby steps towards our objective. This is particularly the case when facing large or daunting tasks, where the only sensible way to proceed is to patiently work on small parts of the larger task to help ensure we make steady progress.

Being patient is often the fastest way of achieving success.

Turn down your 'need to move fast' mentality

If you've an impatient personality, where you always want to rush ahead, you need to manage yourself and practise slowing down. Learn to recognize that progress may happen only through being patient – perhaps because the challenge is new, unknown or complex. In these situations, allow yourself to be guided by friends or colleagues who are temperamentally more inclined to take things more slowly.

Create realistic milestones

With large tasks, patiently break down what you have to do into a series of achievable milestones and work towards achieving each of them. As you reach each milestone, take a moment to celebrate and to thank those who are helping you. By patiently working in this way, you have time to frequently review your progress and to adjust your approach depending on what's working and what isn't.

BEWARE OF FIRST IMPRESSIONS

'Don't rush to judge others'

We spend our lives meeting people online or in person and immediately forming opinions about them. This is an age-old human habit and necessity: to ascertain whether a stranger is friend or foe, we've needed to quickly process their words, appearance and body. Are they a threat to our well-being or will they be an ally?

These initial, snap impressions have a big impact on our lives since they influence our future behaviours and attitudes towards people we've just met – the new colleague you instantly like and want to get to know or your new mother-in-law who strikes you as a bit cold and harsh and whom you sense you'll want to avoid spending time with.

Most of the time your swift judgements prove correct – the person really is too stiff, introverted, formal, uptight, sly or selfish. But have you ever been at the receiving end of such snap judgements and felt unfairly labelled? After all, the other person has only spent a few minutes with you and can't possibly have seen the real you, let alone know your story.

There's a very real risk that our rush to judge strangers leads to missed opportunities for new and meaningful relationships. It might close the doors to more understanding, exploration and discovery and risks leaving us more narrow-minded and prejudiced.

I challenge you to stop judging others instantly and be open to the possibilities and experiences that being more patient and open-minded can bring to your relationships and to your entire life.

Taking your time ensures that you don't unfairly judge someone.

Question your assumptions

Sometimes your initial impression won't capture the full picture because of your own filters – your mix of biases, culture, past experiences and personality. How you perceive people in general might be causing you to incorrectly categorize and judge the person you've just met. This applies equally to people you quickly feel a warm connection with as much as it does to when we don't feel instantly drawn to someone.

Go a little deeper

Withhold acting on your gut feelings until you've probed a little deeper and obtained a few more insights. Give the new colleague or neighbour the benefit of the doubt and ask them a few open-ended questions to learn more about them. By looking beyond your first impressions, you may find that your initial reaction was right all along ... or you might be pleasantly surprised.

EMBRACE UNCERTAINTY

'Be agile in the face of volatility'

Today the new normal is that nothing stays stable and normal for long! This is not a new phenomenon, but nowadays it's a reality that is driven home to us almost every day.

We constantly face disruptions, both big and small, that can turn our lives upside down in an instant. Predictable and solid routines and environments have become a thing of the past. We see this happening all around us, whether in the form of unpredictable pandemics and economic downturns or unexpected cost of living crises and technologies suddenly becoming obsolete.

This is about more than simply dealing with change and facing storms, a topic I covered in No. 17. Instead, it's about learning to thrive when things around you are volatile, uncertain and ambiguous. By recognizing and understanding this, you'll be able to develop the necessary mindset and skills to proactively embrace this new normal.

Becoming comfortable with constant changes will help you navigate life's ups and downs.

Learn to thrive in a volatile and uncertain world

Become comfortable with the volatility in your life and in the world – simply expect it and no longer be surprised when something you thought was stable and clear-cut is suddenly turned on its head. Embrace a mindset of being flexible and agile, so that you can more easily adapt as circumstances change. To those around you, you'll be able to role-model positively embracing the volatility that we are all experiencing.

Learn to tolerate things being uncertain and ambiguous by recognizing that many issues and problems aren't clear-cut (and probably never were) and that the answers and solutions are even less so. To help make optimal choices when surrounded by uncertainty, reconcile yourself to making decisions without ever having absolute clarity. And after making such decisions, be ready to review and course-correct more often than you've been used to doing.

Keep abreast of changes

Stay updated about the changing developments in areas that impact you. By being as informed as possible, you'll be in a stronger position to anticipate and make sense of upcoming changes.

KNOW YOUR RELATIONSHIP WITH MONEY

'Create a stable and positive financial mindset'

People often say that money isn't everything, but virtually every aspect of our lives involves money, so understanding our feelings about it is important. Just thinking about money-related matters can bring up intense emotions, in part because our relationship with money connects to our sense of self-worth, security and happiness.

Our beliefs typically come from our parents' relationship with money, as well as from our other childhood and early-adulthood experiences. Through my coaching I observe two main relationships with money:

- One is a mentality that views money as a source of abundance and opportunity, connecting to growth and confidence. It's a mindset that sees opportunities to create and spend money in every situation and believes money will come even when you have very little today.
- The other mentality relates to feelings of scarcity, insecurity and fear. This can express itself as constant worry about having enough, feelings of not being worthy of having money and finding yourself stuck in a downward cycle of anxiety and struggle.

Most of us switch between these mindsets depending on what is happening in our lives. Some people, however, seem to be stuck in one of them – either being blindly optimistic about money or acting as if they'll never have any.

The key is to have a healthy mental relationship with money not only for the sake of your financial well-being but also for your overall satisfaction with life.

Make money your friend and partner.

Put it into action

64

Assess your relationship with money

Take a moment to reflect on your feelings and beliefs about money. By reflecting on the following two questions, you can uncover what money means to you:

- Do you see money as a source of abundance or of scarcity?
- Are you motivated more by fear and worry or by confidence and calmness when thinking about your financial issues, plans and decisions?

Nurture a healthy relationship with money

Well done if you've already got a positive abundance mindset. Always remember, however, to appreciate that money isn't an end in itself – it's simply a means to create a meaningful and fulfilling life. In that sense, money *isn't* everything.

If you diagnose that you have more of scarcity mindset, allow yourself to start feeling gratitude for what you have, rather than focusing on what you lack. Be kind to yourself when it comes to your financial matters and recognize that financial success is a journey, in which roadblocks and setbacks are to be expected.

FIND A BALANCE WITH FAMILY MEMBERS

'Find ways to get along with your family'

As much as you might want to, you cannot choose your family. Maybe you have incredibly close and warm relationships with your parents and siblings – relationships made stronger from having the same DNA – but sadly, conflict, rivalries and disagreements are common as many of us navigate parental tensions, sibling rivalries and other unhealthy family dynamics.

In these situations, remaining connected to family members can feel like an impossible task. The 'solutions' can all seem less than ideal – whether that's by walking away, giving them the silent treatment or engaging in an all-out row.

Furthermore, difficult family members with their own unique characters, beliefs and habits rarely change, even if you politely ask and encourage them to do so. Little wonder that so many family members only come together at weddings, funerals or celebrations like Christmas.

The secret is to learn to live with difficult family relationships and dynamics in a way that both is civil and preserves your sanity and sense of well-being. It can be a never-ending process, requiring that you acknowledge your needs and feelings while exercising a blend of empathy, courage, compassion and willingness to communicate.

Learning how to deal with challenging family members takes effort and courage.

Put it into action

65

Take command of what's under your control

Your physical presence or absence is a key lever you can use when navigating difficult relationships. By accepting or declining invitations to family gatherings, you'll be able to manage your well-being. Your challenge is to manage the expectations of your parents, siblings and relatives who expect you to turn up to events regardless. You'll need clarity and courage when saying no and be ready to explain why you won't be going to a particular family event.

Much of the advice about stepping away from toxic people and creating boundaries (see No. 12) can be equally applied when considering how you cope with tricky family members.

It's OK (and common) to compromise – to spend as little time as possible with challenging family members, but without walking away for good. Hopefully this reduced interaction will be enough to bring you mental calmness and balance.

Unfortunately, given your history together, family members may have a strong mental hold over you and this mental hold can remain even if you no longer see them in person. The secret is to mentally step away from being triggered when you think about them and how they may have treated you in the past. When negative thoughts relating to them come into your head, tell yourself that it's all OK now, that it was in the past and now you're fine.

JUMP SHIP AS AND WHEN IT SUITS

'Change jobs or careers as often as you need to'

Today, the notion of a lifelong career in a single company, field or even industry is over. It's increasingly expected and even viewed as healthy to switch jobs and careers.

Starting afresh is inevitable if you want to stay true to yourself. As you gain new insights, perspectives and experiences, your views about what constitutes meaningful work and a desirable working environment will evolve. As a result, switching job roles and careers might be your only way of ensuring that your working life remains as rewarding and motivating as possible. Changing roles is also inevitable given the constant emergence of new job roles as old ones disappear.

Once you recognize that your working life will be made up of a series of different job and career opportunities, you can break free from traditional notions of loyalty and commitment. Loyalty to your own growth will now take precedence over blind allegiance to a company or industry. The ideal is to be super loyal and dedicated to a job while you're in it, but free to move on at any time to pursue new opportunities.

Learning to switch jobs as and when you need to is an important skill.

Give yourself regular career coaching

Your overall goal is to create a flexible career path that continually adapts and aligns with the authentic you as you evolve and change.

- Make time to evaluate your interests, values and goals, asking yourself how they have changed since you last thought about them. Think through how well your current job role and workplace align with them and how motivated you feel by your present career.
- Be ready to explore new career paths when you feel the gap between where you are now and your aspirations is growing too wide. You'll know that a gap is emerging when you feel your work is becoming boring, dull, repetitive, meaningless or no longer challenging enough and/or you no longer find your manager and work environment enjoyable or inspiring.
- Know which of your skills and experiences are transferable and can be leveraged in a different industry or role. In addition, identify the skills you lack that would enable you to move into a new field of work. Be ready to learn these skills while also spending time building up professional connections in that field.

BE HAPPY WITH YOUR OWN COMPANY

'Practise being alone'

We all need to spend time by ourselves for the good of our well-being and growth. Sadly, in the hustle and bustle of life it can be hard to make time to be alone. Those around you may not even be willing to leave you alone.

Spending time alone is not about isolating yourself and avoiding social interactions, it's a positive state enabling you to:

- reconnect with yourself without the distractions and demands of other people
- look inside, reflect and gain clarity on your experiences, emotions, thoughts and aspirations
- deepen your understanding of who you are, what you like, need and value, and what brings you fulfilment
- develop independence and self-reliance, as you become less dependent for your happiness on other people's time, attention, validation and presence
- discover a level of peace and contentment that comes from within ourselves, rather than relying on external stimuli and other people to provide it.

The biggest benefit of being comfortable with your own company is that it can paradoxically help you thrive in close relationships with other people. This is because you're less likely to over-depend on them for meaning and happiness, allowing your relationships to be more mature and balanced.

Spending time by yourself is a cost-effective solution to so many of life's problems.

Put it into action

67

Plan time alone

When was the last time you chose to spend a few hours or even days by yourself with no one else for company? Start setting aside time in your diary for 'me time'. Introverts will find this easier to do, since they're temperamentally more inclined to be OK with their own company and will have spent more time alone than a typical extrovert (see No. 9 for a reminder of these personality differences).

Do things alone

Explore taking up activities and hobbies that you can do alone in which you'll be free to be and express yourself. This is very important for our well-being. Such activities include cycling, walking, travelling, reading, gardening or painting. If you're in relationship, take time to communicate your need to sometimes be alone.

Switch off your devices

Being by yourself and using your smartphone is cheating since you're not really alone. Totally unplug and disconnect by turning off your devices. You will feel an invigorating sense of liberation.

BREATHE THROUGH DIFFICULT DAYS

'I find some days are so hard to get through'

Large parts of our lives are filled with dull routines and ordinary struggles – days made up of nothing but traffic jams, monotonous meetings, crying children, annoying colleagues, uninspired meal preparation and other repetitive tasks. These are days that test our patience and composure and ones we're only too happy to forget (and probably very quickly!).

Rather than allowing them to bring us down, it's important to acknowledge that monotonous and challenging days are part of life. Even the richest, happiest and wisest people have such days; no one can escape them. By recognizing this truth, you can learn to navigate them with a more positive and healthy mindset – where you can approach every mundane or annoying task as an opportunity to practise letting go, remaining calm, showing resilience and even treasuring the everyday.

Working through difficult days is an important skill to practise.

Create or find moments of joy

Don't underestimate the importance of making time for positive breaks and activities. Even the dullest of days can be brightened up with small pleasures such as having a nice lunch, taking a quick walk outside, or listening to the radio.

Be kind to yourself

Difficult days are not your fault and you mustn't take them personally – they're simply part of life. They will pass, so there's no point in beating yourself up or getting upset. Instead, speak to yourself with the same understanding and kindness that you would show to a friend facing a similarly challenging day.

Go to bed and do a morning reset

Luckily, no matter how horrible or unmemorable your day has been, you can fall asleep and let the day become history. The following morning, spend a few minutes counting your blessings and being grateful for the small positive things you have in your life.

When you know you have a difficult or dull-as-dishwater day ahead of you, set yourself some positive intentions to help you approach mundane or annoying tasks with a healthy mindset.

EXPLORE YOUR FEARS

'Identify and face your fears'

We all have fears and I don't just mean the obvious, 'classic' ones such as being afraid of spiders, heights or the dark. Through my coaching work, I've explored many types of fears or phobias that my clients carry with them – fear of ...

- failure
- success
- being alone
- pain
- disappointing others
- not making the right choices
- being forgotten
- being unhappy
- not being valued or recognized
- being the centre of attention
- speaking in public
- not doing things perfectly
- growing old
- dying

Such fears are caused by all sorts of things such as childhood trauma, low self-confidence, limiting beliefs, or simply not liking things that seem scary or push us out of our comfort zone.

We don't normally address and deal with our fears well, often because they're embarrassing or feel like a sign of weakness. But not all fears are a bad thing. Many are trivial and have little impact on us, so can be ignored – a fear of spiders or snakes might be an example. Some fears may serve as useful warnings or reminders – a fear of making financial losses, for example, might prompt you to be prudent when making business decisions.

Other fears, however – the ones we need to face up to and overcome – are those that impact negatively on you and your ability to be successful – perhaps it's your fear of upsetting others, making presentations, standing out from the crowd, or flying.

Befriending your fears is a challenging but very fulfilling process to work through.

Create an inventory

Take a moment to identify and list your fears. Divide them into three groups:

1. those that seem trivial and can to all intents and purposes be ignored
2. those that might be helping you
3. those that are holding you back from achieving your full potential.

It's the third group you need to be concerned with.

Face your fears

It's time to stop ignoring or denying those fears that are holding you back and start addressing what is causing them and how to eliminate their paralysing effects.

Many of these fears are irrational and are easily explained:

- You realize you fear being in water because your mother never learned to swim and was afraid of drowning, a fear she passed on to you by discouraging you from going in the sea.
- You fear change because your parents separated when you were a toddler and you seek to avoid any more traumatic changes in your life.

The best way to address these fears is by exposing yourself to them in small, manageable doses that don't overwhelm you. Take a few short flights to help overcome your fear of flying, for example, or ask your boss whether you can make a short presentation in the next departmental meeting to help you face your fear of being in the spotlight.

With some deeply held fears – often linked to childhood traumas and other traumatic experiences – you may struggle to overcome them by yourself. They sometimes come from negative or self-limiting beliefs about yourself and your abilities, such as believing you can never be successful. A therapist or counsellor could help you unearth their root causes and find ways of overcoming them.

ROLE-PLAY THE IDEAL YOU

'Be the better version of yourself'

Becoming the best version of yourself can take time and you can easily find excuses to delay or give up on your self-improvement journey. Thankfully, you can speed up the process by emulating those qualities and behaviours you're aspiring to master – a little like the idea of faking it until you make it.

By intentionally and repeatedly role-playing traits and habits that don't yet come naturally to you, your brain's wiring and muscle memory will evolve, helping these desired qualities become second nature to you. By consciously and patiently exhibiting the mindset and behaviours of the ideal you, your character and personally will begin to embody those qualities.

- By repeatedly remembering to smile, express interest in and act warmly with those around you, you'll turn you into a more caring and empathic person.
- By forcing yourself to regularly speak up in discussions and meetings, while acknowledging and building on other people's ideas, you will bring out your more extrovert and collaborative side.

Practise being the person you want to become.

Put it into action 70

Start with one quality

Think about the gap between your ideal self and how you are today and choose one important quality that you are struggling to master. Maybe it's something others complain that you lack or which visibly upsets people.

Starting with this one quality, create an intention to practise and perform it every single day. It might be making an effort to always listen and appreciate other people's ideas and opinions. Check in with yourself each week to review your progress and also ask for other people's feedback to discover whether they've noticed you exhibiting the new quality or behaviour.

Once you see this is working, start role-playing other habits and behaviours that don't come easily to you.

Have external role models

It may help if you have someone as a benchmark to emulate – a family member who exhibits the selflessness you aspire to or a colleague who shows your desired levels of persistence and diligence. As you copy or mirror their style or attribute, bear in mind that we're all unique and how another person demonstrates a quality such as empathy, being innovative or working smart may not exactly align with how you need to do it.

KNOW WHEN TO COMPROMISE

'Don't dig in your heels'

Every day we encounter situations where we must choose between asserting our needs and desires versus being accommodating.

- You cannot agree with your boss about a deadline for completing a key task – do you simply agree to what she's demanding or do you hold firm and risk upsetting her?
- You cannot agree on your family's holiday plans – your partner wants a beach holiday in Spain while you're keen to have a driving holiday across the US. Will you give in and go to the beach, hold firm or find a compromise solution?

We all have patterns in how we typically respond to differences and disagreements. Some of us always speak up, hold firm and never want to give in, while others are more willing to be flexible and to flow with other people's ideas and actions.

Compromising may feel like a weakness, but it's actually a sign of maturity since it requires an ability to be open and flexible, to listen with a willingness to see other people's points of view and understand their actions and motivations. By choosing to compromise you maintain relationships and create trust, and win-win outcomes may well emerge.

Sometimes, of course, compromise is not the solution: when you need to stand up for your beliefs and values or to defend your and others' boundaries, for example. The secret is to read each situation well enough so that you can decide between being assertive and being flexible and thereby achieve the optimal outcome.

You cannot fight every battle – it's exhausting.

Share your needs and concerns

Listen well and encourage very open and honest dialogue so that both parties know each other's needs, boundaries and concerns. If necessary, pause the discussions until everyone has calmed down and is able to really appreciate each other's feelings and concerns.

Seek common ground

We are very good at spotting differences and at jumping on points of disagreement, but it's harder for us to recognize our areas of agreement and shared interest. Taking the holiday example from the previous page, spend some time finding out where you and your partner are aligned – perhaps you both agree on wanting a fortnight of relaxation, with great food, sunny weather and for a budget of under $4,000. But even after discovering what you have in common, you'll need to be flexible and accommodating if you are to decide between holidaying in the US or in Spain.

Know when to take a stand

While trying to be open and understanding, you need to know when to be assertive and to put a stake in the ground – to share with the other party what's not negotiable and you're not willing to be flexible about. This requires a good understanding of the situation and the other parties, and to think through how your holding firm will impact the relationship.

DON'T BE HALF-ARSED

'Why am I spending my time doing things I hate?'

Have you ever found yourself working through an activity or commitment only to pause and wonder why you're even bothering to do it? It's highly likely that, as a result, you'll only put in the minimal effort and be half-hearted about the whole thing.

Life's far too short to spend time and energy on activities that don't motivate us. But in reality, we all find ourselves stuck with tasks, relationships, careers and 'to do' lists that we're not truly interested in. No matter whether it's a relationship that drains you, a job that depresses you or other tasks that leave you feeling hollow, doing things half-heartedly will eventually leave you feeling unfulfilled and uninspired.

This is no way to live, and the obvious solution is to seek people and tasks that you're able to embrace *whole*heartedly – to help create a personal and professional life that ignites your motivations and passions. But how?

Be all-in or be all-out.

Put it into action

72

Become whole-hearted

Ask yourself which parts of your life don't really inspire or even interest you or leave you feeling apathetic and disinterested. You have two options – continue or stop doing them!

Think through why you're doing each of them. Perhaps they're an acceptable means to an end enabling you to earn money for your future or are obligations that you feel compelled to continue doing. Either way, explore how you could bring your full self to these tasks – you may never feel 100 per cent enthusiastic about them, but at least try to be neutral by not letting them demotivate you.

If it's something that you would like to stop doing, have the courage to make that happen. This isn't easy and will normally involve a combination of saying no, setting boundaries and having some uncomfortable conversations. It may even entail switching jobs or careers, leaving a relationship or totally changing how you spend your time. Some of the advice in this book's other entries, such as on how to walk away in No. 12, can help you navigate these changes.

STOP EXPECTING TO GET SOMETHING IN RETURN

'Give freely and unconditionally'

Giving without expecting anything in return sounds a simple enough premise, but in reality it is neither easy nor common. Typically, most of us have a transactional, score-keeping mentality – always expecting favours in return for our own and watching out for how the other party has responded to our acts of generosity. When we carry this tit-for-tat mentality, we easily become upset when we don't get anything back and the 'rules' of reciprocity aren't applied.

When you allow yourself to give unconditionally, without any strings attached, you free yourself from expecting anything and are no longer attached to the outcome. Your reward is simply to feel fulfilled by giving for its own sake, leaving you with a sense of inner contentment that you've enriched the lives of those around you. By being genuinely unconditional in your giving, you might even set off a chain reaction by encouraging others to 'pay it forward' by copying your selfless act.

It is so cathartic to help other people without any expectation of reward.

Change your beliefs

Starting today, stop expecting reward or recognition for your acts of help and generosity. This won't be easy if you're conditioned to only helping others in return for thanks and recognition. Learn to trust that freely giving will have a positive impact, no matter whether it's recognized or reciprocated. The only outcome that should concern you is how much of a positive impact are you having and how you could do even better next time.

Let people know that you expect nothing in return and feel good with yourself that you can make a positive difference in people's lives without them feeling any pressure to respond in kind.

Seek out opportunities to give freely

Don't wait for moments where you can give your support, time or resources to help others. Instead, proactively seek out opportunities to give a helping hand or be a shoulder to cry on. Offer your time to a local charity, mosque, church, community centre or school.

If others are bemused by your quixotic behaviour, explain that you're helping others unconditionally and then you'll hopefully inspire others to also act without expecting anything in return.

KNOW HOW YOU THINK

'I often kick myself for making terrible decisions'

Understanding and managing how you think is essential to creating a successful life, but sadly few of us master this skill. Indeed, most of us are poor thinkers – these examples will probably resonate with you:

- You reach a conclusion just because it feels good without basing it on all the available information.
- You make a decision based on what has worked before without realizing things have changed.
- You agree with everyone else in the meeting because others think it's the right course of action.
- You choose a way forward based on the initial information you received without giving equal weight to new and more relevant data.
- You seek information to help justify a decision you've already made.

The way you think impacts every one of your actions and choices, no matter whether it relates to your relationships, career or other parts of your life. The ideal is to ensure that every decision you make is rational and well informed and to avoid two very common mistakes:

1. Sticking with a decision simply because you've already invested in it, being overconfident about what you know or can do and over-relying on information that feels comfortable even though it's wrong. These flawed ways of thinking are often referred to as cognitive biases.
2. Lazy and superficial thinking from not being detailed and critical enough when evaluating information – such as not reading all available details, failing to join the dots between pieces of information, or being unable to discern fact from fiction.

Invest time when making key decisions to ensure you'll be happy with the choices you make.

Put it into action

74

Know your biases

Get into a regular habit of observing how you make decisions to try to spot any unhealthy patterns and assumptions. Learn about some common biases such as availability bias and confirmation bias to help you know if you're guilty of them.

Before committing to any choices and decisions, ask yourself some probing questions such as:

- Have I taken into account all the appropriate information?
- Have I faced similar decisions before and how is this influencing me now?
- Are other people influencing my thinking – in a good or bad way?
- Am I choosing a course of action only because I like it, not because it's right?

Think more critically

Invest more time and effort than you normally do when reviewing and evaluating information and upcoming decisions. Sometimes this may take only a few extra minutes and at other times a few hours, but it's better to slow down and make a more considered decision than to rush in and later be left to clean up the consequences of a bad one.

Don't always take information and assumptions at face value and when unsure, seek more evidence. In addition, stay open-minded for longer. This will give you the time to consider alternative options and perspectives before reaching any conclusions. This could entail involving others so you can compare their thinking with your own.

BIDE YOUR TIME

'Don't expect the universe to play into your hands'

Life has a habit of following its own flow, sometimes clashing with our best-laid plans and goals. As a result, when things don't work out for us, we can feel that the universe is conspiring against us.

In a weird way it is, to the extent that things don't always flow as we want. These are the moments when life seems almost to be sending us a message that this may not be our time. The annoying setbacks, the bad news and irritating delays seem to be saying: today is just not your day.

While this can be disappointing, and even leave you feeling depressed, recognizing that timing can be out of your hands can help with your stress levels and well-being. You're now able to stop being obsessed about achieving everything on your terms and in your timeframe and instead become open to the flow of life. 'For everything there is a season, and a time for every matter under heaven,' as the Book of Ecclesiastes wisely tells us.

Learn to let go of expecting events to follow your desired timing.

Put it into action

75

Have faith in the flow of life

Trust that the universe has a plan for you, even if it's not clear and visible to you now. Know that everything happens for a reason and with every setback you have the opportunity to reassess and reformulate how you move forward.

Use any setback to fine-tune your mindset

See every unexpected setback as another reminder to focus on the present, rather than worrying about how your future plans have been upended and how you'll adjust. It's an opportunity to develop your resilience. This might include practising being calm and patient while also allowing yourself to become more adaptable and flexible.

CELEBRATE OTHER PEOPLE'S WINS

'Feel happy for others' success, particularly when they've done better than you'

Doesn't it feel good when people show genuine happiness about your success and accomplishments? When others around you rejoice in your triumphs and wins, it's a wonderful example of empathy, maturity and kindness. We may raise a wry laugh when we hear American novelist William Faulkner's quip about dying a little every time a friend succeeds, but in reality there's nothing much to emulate or praise in this attitude.

Being generous with our praise should be everybody's default response when family, colleagues, friends, neighbours and even strangers accomplish something. Sadly, too many people view life as a competition and are consumed with selfish envy – often struggling to even pretend they're happy by saying 'well done' with a smile. Even worse, when they feel that someone else's success has come at their own expense, they may show themselves to be sore losers, eaten up by other people's achievements.

It'll be no surprise that my advice to you is to embrace a mindset of generosity – to always be genuinely happy for others and to be a great loser. To celebrate another person's success without feeling insecure and jealous doesn't cost you anything and it can enhance your own life in so many ways – fostering in you a sense of positivity, abundance and inspiration, while also endearing you to the person you've just praised.

Being happy for other people is key to a happy life.

Just do it

Regardless of how you feel about another person's success, practise following this very simple process:

- When you become aware of somebody's success, no matter how small the accomplishment, don't stay silent. Be quick, instead, to express your congratulations, finding some warm words in a message or in person. Ensure your congratulatory smile looks genuine and open.
- Reinforce your initial praise with a follow-up sharing of congratulations among your peer group, perhaps by email or in a meeting.
- Show sincere interest in what they've achieved by starting up a conversation around what they did to be successful, how they feel about it and how they plan to build on it. You may learn something, too, after all.

Even if you're normally an envious person, by intentionally repeating this process a few times you'll begin to change how your brain works and you'll find that being generous will become second nature.

MANAGE YOUR ONLINE PRESENCE

'Look out for your digital footprint'

In today's digitally connected world, your online activity and presence are probably larger than your physical ones. From social media, emails, virtual reality and message apps, through to gaming platforms, podcasts and online accounts and payments, we're spending more and more of our lives online.

On the positive side, playing, working and socializing online offers us a vast variety of ways to interact with our fellow human beings, and all from the comfort of our smart devices and laptops. On the negative side, there's a growing list of online-related risks that we must protect ourselves against:

- cyberbullying
- trolling
- spamming
- grooming
- hacking
- phishing
- identity theft
- money scams
- fake accounts and websites
- data theft
- surveillance
- malware.

Our online activities have real-world consequences, making it even more important that you take extra care with your online presence and activities. Better to invest time and effort now, rather than have to deal with the stress of falling for an online scam or having your social media account hacked.

Treat your online presence with the same care and attention you give your physical presence.

Put it into action

77

Be a little paranoid

Pause and reflect about what you do and post online and question *everything*. Do you have any unused accounts and apps that should be cancelled or deleted? Do you really need to give all your personal data when filling in an online form, or can you answer some questions with fake information instead?

Protect yourself and your loved ones

Take seriously how you protect yourself online. As a minimum:

- ensure you've optimized your privacy settings on all the social media accounts, phone apps and websites you use
- have appropriate anti-virus software on your laptop, ensure your passwords are hard to guess and are regularly changed, and enable two-factor authentication whenever available
- be vigilant about what you say and post online and assume it'll remain there forever – people are losing job offers because of old inappropriate social media posts
- be alert to fake people, emails, posts and websites – if in doubt, delete and don't respond
- hold back from turning on your video when meeting new people online and be careful what data you share with them
- treat unexpected emails carefully and be on the lookout for those that appear to be from someone you know when in fact they're not.

BE AN EVERYDAY INFLUENCER

'Convince and persuade – don't force the issue.'

Successfully influencing and convincing others can make a really positive difference in all areas of your life – from persuading your daughter to study harder, negotiating a salary increase with your boss, through to convincing your partner to switch to an electric car and getting colleagues to buy into your new idea.

It's not about forcing others to do what you want. Effective influencing is about winning others over through having a compelling story and vision and seeking to align your needs and interests with theirs. It's about winning over people's hearts and minds and when you do this well, you create amazing win-win outcomes for yourself as well as for those you live and work with.

Winning people over to your ideas and thinking is an important skill that can be learned.

Put it into action

78

Be someone that others want to help

If you'd like people to agree to your requests and needs, make sure they like, respect and trust you first. They need to see you as someone who listens, has empathy and is kind and helpful. The logic of this advice is easy to understand if you put yourself in their shoes – wouldn't you be more open to listening to a colleague's or friend's requests if you liked and trusted them already?

Know what you're talking about

Before asking others to help you in any way, ensure you're clear on:

- what exactly you'd like them to do
- why you're asking them specifically
- how you think or expect them to respond to your request
- how you'll counter any reluctance on their part to agree to what you're asking.

Communicate well what you want

No matter whether you're asking in person or via an email, ensure your wording is clear and will resonate with those you want to win over. Use compelling messages and stories and highlight the benefits and value of agreeing to your request.

In addition, think through the ideal timing and form of your message – this might mean waiting for when your partner or boss is in a good mood, or pausing until you're face to face rather than asking them by SMS or email.

Understand the other party

If your partner or team member pushes back and says no to what you're asking, take time to appreciate their reluctance and concerns. Explore what their motivations and interests are and take tips from No. 72 about how to compromise and find a win–win solution. Maybe you can agree to a compromise where they will help you, but not exactly in the way you'd originally hoped.

DEPLOY HUMOUR AND LAUGHTER

'I think I'm too serious and need to loosen up'

Sharing and inspiring moments of laughter is the solution to many of life's problems. Being able to laugh is a simple reminder that we mustn't take our lives or ourselves too seriously and that moments of joy can arise even during the most stressful of days.

Laughing causes our bodies to release endorphins, better known as the feel-good hormones. These lift our spirits, reduce our stress, improve our immune system and foster our overall well-being. What's more, laughing with others brightens up everybody's mood and helps facilitate more effective and open communication and relationships.

Sadly, we don't laugh enough. You often see this when taking the train, sitting in the office or walking down the street, where people's unwillingness to laugh or even smile might suggest most of us are taking life too much in earnest. It's time you loosened up by regularly breaking into laughter. It'll be great for your health and will foster success in every area of your life.

Laughing each day can open the door to all kinds of positive outcomes.

Put it into action

79

Laugh at yourself

Stop taking things, including yourself, too seriously. When feeling burdened, stressed or overwhelmed by things not going to plan, take a moment to step back and laugh. Laugh at yourself for worrying too much, for forgetting that life is so short and that in the bigger scheme of things most of it doesn't matter that much. Your laughing should help lighten your mood and help you put everything into a more balanced and positive perspective.

If you're out of practice and find it hard to loosen up, seek out some fun activities to help break the ice – play games with your kids, start a team meeting with a daft activity, go to the pub with colleagues and share jokes, or pay a visit to your local comedy club.

Seek out and spend time with fun and positive people in your personal or working life, allowing their positivity to rub off on you.

Create laughter around you

Once you've got into the habit of laughing and having fun, share these positive feelings and that energy with those around you. Whether over dinner with family or coffee with colleagues, be the one who starts the fun storytelling and sharing of jokes.

BE AS CURIOUS AS THE PROVERBIAL CAT

'Ask questions and ask again'

In all parts of our lives, from our close relationships through to our professional lives, being curious ensures we grow and avoid stagnating. It helps us to innovate, do things differently and discover new opportunities and ways of doing things.

Curiosity links to having a childlike sense of wonder, of wanting to understand and make sense of the world around us. Some of us are born more naturally open and inquisitive than others, but thankfully it's a mindset that we can all practise and develop. By doing so we broaden our perspectives, deepen our understanding of everything around us and uncover new ways of achieving our goals.

The skill that comes naturally to every curious person is to ask questions and to pause to ensure understanding. The power of asking probing, insightful and left-field questions cannot be stressed enough. This links to stopping yourself from launching into anything before you've fully understood the relevant issues, circumstances and options.

Asking questions will help you better understand any kind of situation or person.

Put it into action

80

Develop a curious mindset

Approach all new experiences with a sense of curiosity and a willingness to look around and probe a little. To not accept things at face value or after they've been explained to you only once. Instead, make the time and courage to dig a little deeper by raising the questions that you feel need asking – sometimes it might be to clarify a point and at other times to force a deeper understanding of an issue.

Challenge assumptions

Don't leave stones unturned if you sense there's more to learn and explore. And know it's healthy to question preconceived notions and assumptions, even when you're the only one doing the questioning and it makes others feel you don't trust them. So many of the problems and issues in our world are occurring because prejudices and assumptions aren't being challenged.

Read voraciously

Nurture your curious mindset by continually reading, studying and learning, and apply the advice given in No. 46 to help you become a continuous and lifelong learner.

DIVE EVEN DEEPER

'Explore your potential as far you can'

Discovering your true abilities and potential is essential if you want to achieve everything you're capable of. Unfortunately, very few people ever find out and instead underestimate their capabilities and never discover their untapped potential. It's as if they're free-diving in the sea and come up for air too early without ever realizing they're capable of holding their breath for longer and exploring even deeper.

It's so easy to think we're not capable of doing more, and by just thinking this we stop ourselves from even trying to explore what more might be possible. Children are a joy to watch since they've no idea of what's possible and not possible, so unlike adults they don't hold themselves back by creating limiting beliefs.

It's so incredibly powerful to believe that more might be possible and then to allow yourself to go and find out – at work, as a parent, in a relationship or simply within yourself. By discovering your untapped potential, you'll grow in confidence, more easily leave your comfort zones and set more ambitious goals for yourself.

No. 48 encouraged you never to settle and this entry builds on that advice by encouraging you to proactively explore how far you can go, how deep you can free-dive. The alternative is to never know or to find out too late in life. Why wait when you can get started now!

You will never know how far you can go, until you try.

Forget what you thought was possible

Stop being one of those people who at a nightclub spends the entire time sitting in the corner claiming they're not a good dancer or cannot dance at all. If you have any desire to create a better future for yourself, then stop having such limiting beliefs. Stop quoting them to other people and stop saying them to yourself. Change your inner dialogue so that it's about you being open to possibility and asking, 'I wonder what I'm really capable of ... Let's find out.'

Set stretch goals

To help you move beyond your previous mental limits, create some ambitious yet achievable new goals. Called 'stretch goals', these targets will give you something to work towards and motivate and inspire you to dive deeper than you ever thought possible.

Your stretch goals can be created for any part of your life:

- running half marathons faster
- completing reports to a higher quality
- leading a bigger team successfully
- becoming a public speaking expert
- being a more confident dancer
- becoming an award-winning chef
- being more comfortable in a permanent relationship
- winning a job promotion
- being more patient and persistent.

The worst that can happen is that you fail miserably. More likely, though, is that you'll probably surprise yourself and discover that, even if you missed the target you created, you'll still have set a new personal best.

SIMPLIFY YOUR LIFE

'Ditch the clutter'

It's very easy to live lives that quite literally overflow with physical possessions, obligations and distractions. In my coaching I come across this all the time:

- A woman with at least a hundred pairs of shoes has no space to store anything else and so is told by her partner, 'Enough is enough.'
- A young man shows me his smartphone to prove he really does have over 200 downloaded apps.
- A writer I'm mentoring misses an email from me and blames this on the fact she receives a few hundred emails per day. Later she shows me her inbox brimming with useless emails from companies and products she's signed up to or expressed an interest in.
- A product designer points to her calendar, bemoaning the fact that due to back-to-back meetings, she doesn't have a single free space in that week's diary.
- A recently appointed head of a not-for-profit confesses he's on the board of half a dozen other companies and gets confused over which paperwork relates to which company.

Sometimes, I feel exhausted just thinking about these people's situations! But we all have similar examples of clutter in our lives, whether it's physical or mental. Holding on to it all might be an addiction, may bring you comfort, or even make you feel important, but no matter how you justify having so much stuff, it's not a healthy way to live.

Embracing simplicity is the way forward. This doesn't mean throwing everything away or cancelling every engagement; it's about purposefully letting go of things that bring no real value or benefit. By seeking simplicity, you create physical and mental space for yourself, freeing you up to concentrate on what really matters in your life.

Simplifying your life frees up mental and physical space that is so liberating.

Put it into action

82

Seek quality over quantity

Adopt a 'less is more' mindset by no longer seeing the acquisition of things and appointments as a positive badge of honour. Just because you have a full diary of meetings, cupboards stuffed with new clothes, a large pile of unread books by your bed or a packed social calendar doesn't make you a successful, happy person. Instead, start to keep tabs on and appreciate what you truly need and value. Ask yourself whether you really need that new pair of brogues, the latest prize-winning novel or yet another position on a board.

Physically declutter

The process of sorting through your things and purging what you no longer need is cathartic and liberating. This might involve:

- throwing away those out-of-date herbs and spices in your kitchen cupboard
- tidying up what you keep in your office drawers
- downsizing to a smaller apartment
- getting rid of an unused second car
- going online to sell half of your wardrobe.

Hopefully a lot of this stuff won't end up in landfills. Try to find new homes for all your discarded belongings by selling them or by giving them to charity, family or friends.

Mentally declutter

Take some time to explore which tasks, activities and thoughts can be eliminated. This will help you reduce what your brain needs to remember and focus on.

- Can you work less and take on fewer tasks – fewer trips, meetings, projects, etc.?
- Can your holidays be pared back, with time spent on a quiet beach rather than on a breakneck tour of three countries?
- Do you really need four credit cards and/or multiple online bank accounts?
- Could you become more mindful by letting go of unnecessary worries and concerns that might be filling your head?

PUT ON YOUR OWN OXYGEN MASK FIRST

'Don't always put other people's needs ahead of your own'

In our busy lives, it's very easy to discover we're helping other people while forgetting about ourselves. Juggling work and family matters can leave you with little energy or time for your own needs.

Neglecting yourself may appear kind and selfless, but eventually it will reduce your capacity and motivation to do anything – including helping others. By giving yourself time to care for yourself, you'll maintain your energy and motivation levels, allowing you to more impactfully support those around you.

Putting on your own metaphorical oxygen mask first is a wise act of self-compassion. Never allow other people to make you feel guilty when they say that putting yourself first is selfish. It's simply you valuing yourself and recognizing that by looking after yourself, you're better equipped to face all your challenges and obligations – sustainably.

Looking after your own needs before those of others is essential to your well-being.

Five tips to put yourself first

- Watch yourself closely: recognize when you're feeling overwhelmed and need to step back and give yourself some 'me time'.
- Be as kind to yourself as you are to others. Show the same compassion and empathy that you offer to those close to you.
- Block times in your daily routine for yourself, times that you make non-negotiable and won't easily cancel. Use these times to replenish and rejuvenate yourself – read, meditate, walk, go to the gym or have a massage.
- Protect your well-being by being willing to turn down requests to do things that will drain you. Avoid allowing other people to emotionally blackmail you into giving them your time and energy when you feel it will only bring you down.
- Just as others seek you out when they need some extra help and support, do likewise by approaching others when you need to offload and open up.

APPRECIATE THE PRICELESS THINGS IN LIFE

'Remember, a loving smile is worth a thousand swanky cars'

It's very easy to equate success and happiness with what we own and what we're able to buy. So many of our behaviours and habits perpetuate this belief – such as our obsession with celebrities, watching reality-TV shows and being addicted to social media.

Having money is obviously important, since so much in our lives needs to be paid for – the food on our plate, a roof over our head, getting around. But you'll never find genuine happiness and fulfilment in your life if you fail to appreciate the many valuable things that come without a price tag.

When looking back and reflecting on their lives, dying people don't talk about how happy they were owning a three-bedroom house, driving a succession of luxury cars or having a large pension scheme. No, it's the things that money couldn't buy that form their fondest memories, such as:

- the warmth of a partner's smile
- the love between them and their family members
- the beauty of a sunset or view from a hilltop
- enjoying inner peace
- time with their children
- laughter and fun moments with friends
- feeling valued and appreciated
- not being stressed or anxious
- being in nature.

It's these priceless gifts that make our lives more fulfilling and meaningful. By pausing to appreciate them, you'll have so much joy, purpose and happiness in your life, regardless of your financial circumstances.

Learning to appreciate and value the free things in life will bring you untold joy.

Put it into action

Change your thinking

Learn to appreciate the simple pleasures in life, things that to date you may have overlooked or seen as trivial. To realize their immense value, be mindful and fully present when doing them – whether you're listening to music, having a cup of tea with friends, reading a great book or eating with loved ones.

Enjoy being in nature

Spending time outdoors and enjoying the natural world offers you joy and well-being at little cost – you might choose to walk in a local park, trek in a forest or bathe in the sea. No. 93 provides more insights about the importance of being in nature.

Value friendships

Spend your time with people who energize and inspire you. Remember that developing and maintaining meaningful relationships may take your time and attention, but it doesn't need to cost you any money.

Seek free knowledge

Knowledge is an amazingly valuable thing that, thanks to the internet, is increasingly freely available. It's possible to learn and to develop yourself without paying anything – whether it's watching self-help videos on YouTube, taking free online business courses, or visiting your local library.

ADDRESS UNSPOKEN ISSUES

'Point out the elephant in the room'

We've all been guilty of ignoring issues in our lives – situations that we're acutely aware of but prefer not to talk about and acknowledge, let alone tackle and solve. These so-called 'elephants in the room' come in all shapes and sizes and we ignore them to avoid arguments, tension, discomfort or embarrassment.

Through my coaching work, I've realized these unspoken issues typically relate to bad news or things not going well and fall into a few categories:

- relationship and family challenges
- integrity and ethical issues
- financial struggles and difficulties
- health problems and illnesses
- poor teamworking or leadership
- workplace performance issues
- poor business decisions
- career struggles.

Sometimes they'll resolve themselves, but most of the time ignoring them only makes the situation worse – the financial difficulties grow, relationships break down, poor decisions become more costly ...

It's so easy to avoid addressing them, particularly when you feel it's a group issue and you have no desire to be the one who kicks off an uncomfortable discussion. It takes courage and sometimes desperation but acknowledging that these elephants exist is the first step to being able to resolve them and move on.

Addressing the elephants in the room can clear the air and remove roadblocks in your life.

Put it into action

Understand your part

With any difficult issues, it's very easy to blame others and play the victim card. When there's an 'elephant in the room', ask yourself what has been your part in causing, creating or perpetuating the problem. Be willing to acknowledge this in any later discussions about the issue.

Talk with others about your shared elephants

Have the courage to start the conversation, but before doing so, plan how, with whom and where the tricky issue will be discussed. You may find it easier to talk one-on-one with each family or team member involved, before facilitating a whole-group discussion.

These types of conversation require a psychologically safe environment where people will feel free to open up without worrying about recrimination. Expect difficult emotions and tears to be expressed and for possible finger pointing and blame games. Role-model being calm, empathic and non-judgemental and show you're listening by making comments such as 'I hear you', 'I really understand', 'I feel the same'.

... And resolve them together

No two elephants are exactly the same – each has its own unique combination of context, players, impacts and history. But as a rule of thumb you can optimally solve any of them by:

- being open to outside help – for example, by asking a neutral family member or colleague to help facilitate or mediate
- clearing the air – by giving people time to get over feelings of hurt, blame and anger
- writing down and agreeing a plan of action that defines the ideal outcomes or goals
- making time to recognize and celebrate together when the issue has been successfully worked through.

DO THINGS FOR THE FIRST TIME

'Try out new experiences, hobbies, skills ... new anything!'

Life can easily become routine and monotonous, particularly given our tendency to stay with what we know well and are comfortable with. This can feel safe and predictable, but you'll miss out on the depth and richness that come only from new experiences and trying things out for the first time.

Trying out new experiences and opportunities brings us so many benefits:

- It wakes us up and helps us feel more alive.
- It broadens our horizons and a sense of what's possible.
- It keeps us on our toes and makes life exciting.
- It injects energy and enthusiasm into our lives.
- It helps us uncover new passions and purpose to our lives.
- It builds up our confidence to embrace change.
- It opens us up to new insights, learning and discoveries.
- It encourages us to become more innovative, creative and adaptable.

Doing anything new can feel scary, daunting and difficult, but the positives almost always outweigh the downsides. So, what are you waiting for? It's time for you to seek out something new!

Becoming a regular 'first-timer' will energize you.

Work through your 'first-time' bucket list

Take time to create a list of all the possible activities and experiences that interest you but which you've never tried before. Maybe you've never even thought about them or perhaps you have but for whatever reason didn't give them a go.

When creating your list, think about the situations when you feel bored, complacent or stagnated. It is in these areas that you should be seeking out new experiences. If you find exercising at home is becoming monotonous, try out a kickboxing or Zumba class; if you're tired of beach holidays, find a completely new way of spending your vacation time.

Once you have created your list, use it as a guide that you want to work through, ticking off things as you experience them. If you're feeling a bit daunted about jumping into something totally new, try sampling the new experience first by taking a trial Zumba class or adding a mountain hike to your regular beach holiday. As you gain more confidence, you can allow yourself to take on more significant new experiences.

Given how much courage and effort it may have taken, remember to pause and pat yourself on the back when you've successfully tried out something for the first time.

MAKE OTHERS FEEL GOOD ... AND DO GOOD

'Have a positive impact on other people'

No matter how busy and focused you are on your own issues and goals, never forget to help and support other people. The simple act of being there for others is one of the most profound and meaningful roles that any of us can perform. When we all act in this way it brings us together and its benefits extend beyond one helpful act. By being genuinely altruistic and kind, you set in motion some amazing ripple effects:

- Your acts of kindness release feel-good hormones that help you feel more positive and less stressed.
- Through the concept of karma (covered in No. 27), you'll find people around you becoming more open to helping you in return – more willing to be there for you when you need an extra pair of hands, some positive feedback, or someone to listen to your problems.
- Your example will make those around you more inclined to be generous to the people in their lives.

Always be there for other people.

Put it into action

87

Seek ways to help

Every day, be open and proactive in offering your time and positive words to anyone who seems to be in need. Regularly ask people, 'How can I be of help?' The help you bring might be as small as making someone a coffee or passing them their post. But sometimes it might involve doing something more substantial, such as driving a neighbour to their hospital appointment or working over the weekend to help an overburdened colleague with an urgent task.

Be randomly helpful and kind

Help people who least expect it and do so in random ways – perhaps it's giving a box of chocolates to a helpful neighbour or a bunch of flowers to a colleague simply to say thank you for all that they do.

Freely help without expectation

Remember the advice given in No. 73 about being generous and helpful without any expectation of getting something in return? Give your time, energy and resources to others simply for the pleasure of bringing joy and positivity to their day.

DEVELOP AN EARLY-WARNING SYSTEM

'Don't be ambushed by what life throws at you'

We can be so caught up in the present moment that we forget to look ahead in a proactive way. We keep our heads down and fail to appreciate upcoming obstacles, possible crises or developing opportunities.

This is totally understandable given that just getting through the day might take all your time and energy. The secret is to focus on the present while having a proactive mindset – a mindset that's ready to look ahead to foresee and navigate any ups and downs along your path. It's about being one step ahead to avoid being caught by surprise. It's emulating the chess player who's always thinking a few moves ahead.

By acting in this way you'll face fewer shocks and stressful surprises – fewer moments of 'If only I'd stopped for a moment and thought ahead a bit more'. When any surprises do occur, you'll have a better chance of being prepared and be able to flex and adapt accordingly.

Keeping an eye on the future and what might happen can help you avoid untold difficulties.

Learn to scan the horizon

Anticipating what may happen in our personal and professional lives will never be an exact science and no one tool will suit every situation. But as a general rule, keep your eyes open and gather intelligence to spot signs of what changes that might be around the corner – a relationship breaking down, a client becoming uncomfortable with your service, or your boss dropping you from an important project.

Become a contingency planner

After you've anticipated what might be around the corner, think through your options for responding and your preferred outcome. Are you happy to let the relationship die and move on? Do you want to keep the client at any cost, or remain on that high-profile project?

Once you've chosen a way forward or a response, prepare thoroughly, particularly if you foresee a difficult challenge coming your way. Decide whether it's better to be proactive and respond now or wait until the event happens or the decision is announced before you react.

Make more informed decisions

Use the same skills of looking ahead and anticipating things whenever you're making key decisions. This increases the likelihood that you'll make the optimal decision and not one your future self will regret.

Balance being in the present with looking ahead

Don't lose sight of the present when being proactive and looking to the future. The advice given in No. 10 remains true: focusing on the present is the healthy way to live. Continue being anchored to the here and now, even as you anticipate what might be sailing your way tomorrow.

USE IT OR LOSE IT

'I wish I had maintained that valuable skill'

When we're busy, it's very easy for things to be forgotten or relegated to the bottom of our priorities. Most of the time this might be fine, but it's such a shame if you're neglecting and allowing to go to waste things that you might have spent years working on. This is often the case with skills we've acquired and relationships we've developed.

We might spend years becoming expert in a particular skill or area of knowledge – playing a musical instrument, speaking a second language, becoming expert in family law or financial investing. When we stop practising and using these skills, we weaken a foundation of our success. The longer we neglect that particular talent or expertise, the more difficult it becomes for us to return to our previous levels of proficiency.

It's the same with our relationships. We might have spent years working or building a friendship with someone and together creating high levels of trust and respect, but then we lose touch or don't make enough time for the relationship and it dies, in part because of the idea that 'out of sight is out of mind'.

Sometimes your neglect is OK because you've consciously decided that the skill is no longer needed or you've outgrown the friendship. But what about those forgotten skills and relationships that might be of immense value and meaning to your life? Here I'll share tips for how to get these back.

It's better to maintain your skills rather than to later regret losing them.

Put it into action

89

Prioritize what's truly important

Regularly think through who you risk losing touch with or which skill or area of knowledge you risk forgetting. If you decide you don't wish to lose them, make sure you put them in the high-priority box of your to-do list.

Intentionally practise

Maintaining an expertise doesn't occur by chance. It happens only through regular practice and using the skills on a consistent basis. To avoid neglecting skills, start including time in your weekly diary to practise them or to keep abreast of the latest knowledge.

Maintain the threads of connection

Keep an updated list of those you consider to be (or have been) your good friends and work colleagues. Dedicate time and energy to keeping those relationships alive and in some cases to bringing them back to life by reconnecting. Never allow such relationships to fizzle out unless you intentionally decide that's the right thing to do.

Be proactive and consistent in how you keep in touch – from one-on-one meet-ups and regular messaging through to sending festive greetings cards and inviting people to social or professional events.

Be grateful if it comes back with any effort

You may discover that the skill you've neglected is as retrievable as riding a bicycle and on trying to use it again, find that you're still as proficient as you ever were. Similarly, with friends you've lost touch with, when you finally reconnect you may be surprised that the bond is as strong as ever and that you can pick up from where you left off.

LET YOURSELF GO CRAZY

'Pursue your dreams, however crazy'

Too many people chase success in conventionally sensible ways, focusing on things like personal productivity, working smart and achieving 'serious' goals. This might work for you most of the time, but it's unlikely to leave you feeling exhilarated or exclaiming 'Wow, wow ... wow!'.

At some point we all need to break free of the monotony and predictability of our everyday lives. To step away from normal in search of crazy. At the core of this thinking is the sobering recognition that life is short and our death may never be that far away.

Embracing crazy is about setting yourself audacious and outlandish-sounding goals, about taking unexpected and out-of-character actions and decisions. Let yourself go and do those things that you never expected but always wanted to do – have a relationship with someone 20 years your junior, travel across Africa on a motorbike, train to become a priest, write that novel that's been sitting in your head for years, or become a naturist and sunbathe naked on the beach.

Others will say you've gone crazy, but deep down they'll be in awe and a little envious. Some will even be inspired to seek out their own ways of breaking free and feeling more alive.

Being crazy might be the best way of achieving your dreams.

Put it into action

90

Dream as if the sky's the limit

Ask yourself these questions to work out how you want to break free:

- If anything were possible and there were no constraints, what life goals and dreams would you set for yourself (alone or together with your loved ones)?
- What do you feel is missing in or unfulfilled about your personal and/or professional life?
- Which activities, experiences and relationships do you really wish to try out and pursue?

Once you've written down your answers, think through whether you're ready and able to pursue them. Share them with those you're close to, particularly if you need their help and support or if you want to do them together. Don't tell just anyone, though. To some, your goals might seem reckless or stupid and their criticism or ridicule may send you scuttling back down your 'normal' hole.

Live spontaneously

In addition to pursuing these goals, allow yourself to live more in the moment by embracing unpredictability and spontaneity. No matter how crazy they may seem, start saying 'yes' to invitations and opportunities, particularly those involving new experiences, adventures and people to meet. By spontaneously living in the moment, you might experience levels of joy and happiness you never knew were possible.

Be kind while being crazy

Try to be as understanding and kind as possible with those whose own lives may be disrupted by your plans. They'll probably struggle to understand or like what you're proposing – whether you want to spend months travelling overseas, switch to a low-paying charity career, or give up all your free time to return to studying.

BEFRIEND AI

'Overcome your fears that AI will take away your job and control your life'

Every week in the media we see stories of newly launched artificial intelligence (AI) related tools and solutions that will impact all our lives in one way or another. We're living through a revolutionary time, with experts saying that we're on the cusp of a world in which AI will transform every part of our lives.

The benefits of AI are undeniable – with efficiencies and productivity gains across the board, with AI able to deal with a greater complexity and higher volume of tasks than we're capable of doing ourselves. Everybody I speak to on the subject is excited about the possibilities, but they're also increasingly concerned. We worry that AI will take over our jobs and our lives and we also fear that AI will increasingly invade our privacy and even control us. It doesn't help when global tech leaders warn of AI leading to human extinction!

In spite of these growing concerns, we mustn't simply resist the emergence and impacts of AI. The ideal is to embrace it by focusing our energy and attention on how AI can help make our lives more productive, enjoyable and fulfilling, even while being aware of the potential risks and dangers.

Making friends with AI can help you excel.

Put it into action

View AI as your helpful and positive partner

Adopt a mindset of wanting to discover and enjoy the benefits and positives of AI, while also being mindful of the risks and dangers. Whenever you're presented with an AI-enabled system or app, view it as your potential partner and explore how it can complement, support and build on your own abilities and efforts. Within your team or company, stay ahead of the curve by always embracing the potential benefits that AI might bring to your professional life.

Make time to experiment

Be very open to learning by proactively searching for and trying out AI-enabled tools and systems, even if, on first inspection, they don't appear 100 per cent related to your work or personal needs. You never know what you might discover.

Speak up when AI clashes with your values

While viewing AI with a positive mindset, keep an eye out for AI-enabled tools that might function or be used in ways that go against your values or are unethical. As an example, one of my clients recently shared that his team trialled an online AI-powered recruitment system, only to discover that its software algorithms gave more weight to job seekers whose CVs (resumés) were laid out and formatted in a certain way, even though that bore no relation to the applicants' true abilities and potential.

LET GO OF WHAT YOU FEAR LOSING

'Love what you have – but be prepared to relinquish it with grace and detachment'

It's only natural to feel deeply attached to things you know well and value – whether it's a close relationship, job role, client relationships, daily routines, investments or prized possessions. No sane person ever wants to lose something they've grown comfortable with.

The danger is when our attachment turns into a crippling fear of losing it – perhaps a fear of your partner leaving you, of losing your high-paying job or of not being able to afford the life you have. Some of your fears might feel justified – perhaps because an economic recession is looming or your partner talks of wanting to leave you.

The danger is when a logical worry festers in your head and turns into a paranoid fear that plays havoc with your life. You might be holding on so tightly that your fear turns into reality – your partner feels metaphorically suffocated and leaves you, or you're fired because you were so desperate to be seen as indispensable that you took credit for other people's work.

Moreover, by focusing on retaining what you possess now, you might fail to recognize new and better possibilities – options that might bring you more value and meaning than you currently enjoy.

Being ok losing what you have, leaves you free to truly live life.

Understand what you fear losing

Think through what you worry about losing and ask yourself why you might feel that way.

- Are you worrying about losing your partner because you over-depend on them financially or psychologically?
- Do you fear for your job because it took you months to secure it or because you think you're too old to be back on the job market?

You may never be 100 per cent certain of your motivations, but having even a general sense of why you might be holding on to something is a first step to being able to overcome the fear of losing it.

Detach yourself

The advice given in No. 69 outlines how to work through and overcome any kind of fear and this also applies when you're confronting a fear of letting go. In addition, though, you need to develop a detachment mindset. Being detached involves no longer worrying about what may happen to you if you lose something:

- Be present and do your best now, for example in your job role or marriage, without allowing yourself to become paranoid about what you could lose.
- Develop an abundance mentality – knowing that even if the worst happens, you're confident there are always other ways of earning a living or other people to fall in love with.

Practise being detached by letting go of smaller attachments first and noticing how easy or difficult that is for you. By continually letting go of attachments and not allowing new ones to form, you'll slowly overcome your fear and one day you'll never fear losing anything again.

GO OUTSIDE

'Make time to be in nature'

Thanks to technology and working from home, we're spending too long cooped up indoors, sitting down glued to our screens. This is unhealthy for us in so many ways – in terms of our well-being, stress levels and mental abilities as well as our relationships.

The solution is very simple – spend as much time as possible outside, whether it's simply stepping outside your home or office or travelling to a place where nature is all around you. By doing so, you escape from sitting too much, your eyes aching from too much screen time, being drained by working under artificial light and breathing air that's turning stale.

When you're outdoors you have the uplifting and energizing effects of the sun against your face, the breeze on your skin and the sound of birds singing and falling rain, all while enjoying the beautiful views of trees, hills and flowing water. These outdoor moments help you to unplug, to find peace, calm and greater clarity, and generally lower your stress and anxiety levels. You'll feel so much better about yourself and you'll be a calmer and nicer person to be around.

Being in the countryside is so much more energizing than sitting in your office.

Put it into action

93

Make time in your day

Be determined and intentional about making time to step outside every day, even in cold or rainy weather. It could be just a half hour in a local park or square or an afternoon's walk in a wood or by the sea. The only time you're allowed to stay inside is when the air quality is poor or there's a dangerous storm brewing!

Work outside

Whenever possible, work outside – take your laptop into your garden when joining an online meeting or hold a team meeting outside by walking and talking together in a nearby park. Weather permitting, I find that coaching someone outdoors can boost our shared thinking and creativity.

Even more fulfilling than taking your office outside is to find a career that actually involves you working outside. In addition, try walking or cycling rather than driving or taking public transport whenever you're making short journeys.

Do outdoor stuff

For some, it's natural to spend their free time engaging in outdoor activities, but for others it can feel like a chore. If you belong to the latter camp, double your efforts to arrange outings to the beach or nearby woods, to take daily morning or evening walks and have lunch in your garden or out of the office.

Go outside when upset

When you're feeling upset and angry, at work or at home, stop what you're doing and take a walk or sit outside, even if only for a few minutes. Allow yourself to pause, close your eyes and breathe, staying there until you've calmed down and regained your composure.

Be outside with no tech

When you're outside, even for an hour's lunch break, leave your phone or tablet at your desk. I know it's hard to do, but allow yourself to switch off from your messages and social media and instead simply enjoy being in the moment.

PURSUE YOUR DREAMS WITH CAUTION

'Be prepared to brave the consequences of failure'

At different points in our lives, we find ourselves at a decision-making crossroads: do we keep to the safe path that seems well trodden and safe, or do we take the one that's unknown and risky but which better aligns with our dreams and passions? The former provides security and comfort, while the latter is about chasing your dreams.

This entry builds on the importance of knowing what you're passionate about (see No. 23), as well as never settling for second-best options (see No. 48), by exploring how to pursue your passions when there's a very real risk that you'll fail.

You may worry that you will:

- fail in your desire to start your own business, having walked away from a successful career
- struggle in a new dream job, after leaving a secure one
- find it impossible to keep up mortgage repayments on your dream home, having upgraded from a far cheaper and smaller one.

It would be too simplistic to say that you should simply follow your dreams and, if you fail, learn from what went wrong and try again. I've known too many people who've given up so much to pursue their dreams only to fail and be unable to live with the consequences – becoming broken or clinically depressed, and in one case taking their life.

My advice is twofold:

- Always know that it's better to struggle and fail at pursuing your passions and dreams than to succeed at something that doesn't set your heart on fire, BUT ...
- Pursue those passions and dreams only when you know you can survive the consequences of not succeeding – that you won't be mentally destroyed or crippled by losing your savings, reputation, property, relationships or other important parts of your life.

Be able to live with the risk and cost of failure whenever you're chasing a dream or goal.

Ensure you can live with the downsides

I want you to achieve all your dreams. With your smaller ones, like wanting to complete a travel bucket list, write a book or learn to speak Chinese, you can safely pursue them without worrying too much about the consequences of not succeeding. The worst that can happen is you lose a little money or feel you've wasted some of your time.

With major life choices and decisions, you need to ensure you can live with the impacts of failing and losing what you've given up and invested. To ensure you'll 'live to fight another day'.

To help you make such life-changing decisions:

- List the possible effects if things don't go to plan and work out as hoped.
- Think through how acceptable the impacts of failing would be to you – ask yourself whether the loss of savings or income would be bearable, or whether you'd be OK spending a few months looking for a new job, etc.
- Talk with others who may also be impacted if your plans don't succeed to ensure you're all aligned about what you decide to do.
- Seek advice from anyone who may help you sense-check the impacts of the choices open to you.
- Finally, make your decision about how you'll proceed – either as planned, with adjustments (e.g. taking smaller steps first so as to have smaller downsides), or by delaying (e.g. until you've doubled your financial savings). Shelving your dream altogether is the nuclear option when you conclude that the consequences of not succeeding will be too much to bear.

Beware of overconfidence bias

When we're thinking of chasing our dreams, our excitement and hopes can cloud our judgement. It's important that you don't assume everything will be fine and ignore or downplay the probability and impact of things not going to plan.

DO, MAKE AND REPAIR THINGS YOURSELF

'Become your own odd-job person'

Seeking an easy and convenient life by outsourcing our daily tasks is the new norm. Things that we used to do for and by ourselves we now outsource – from ordering takeout food to having someone fix a leaking tap. We're increasingly washing our hands of the chores that used to form an integral part of our daily routines.

Given how busy our work lives can be, it's understandable that we're tempted to pay others to do the more tedious of our household tasks, leaving us with more time to have fun and to rest. But this convenience culture is causing us to miss out on the satisfaction that comes from making or fixing something with our own hands – that sense of achievement and self-sufficiency that comes from eating food you've prepared yourself, admiring your garden you have looked after, or enjoying a bathroom you've renovated in your spare time.

In addition, by repeatedly relying on others, you'll lose (or never gain) some useful skills such as being able to cook, garden, paint, or do basic plumbing jobs. You risk becoming reliant on others and no longer being in control of the things around you.

It's time to roll up your sleeves and get your hands dirty!

Doing things yourself saves you money, teaches you new skills and is so satisfying.

Do it yourself

Challenge yourself to be more hands-on and self-reliant by not outsourcing everything all the time. You'll save money, boost your skills and self-confidence and appreciate life in a different way when using your hands. It's OK to start small by:

- pausing before ordering another takeaway meal and consider making your own pasta dish or curry tonight
- having your paid gardener come less often, enabling you to occasionally cut the grass, prune the trees or weed the flowerbeds
- changing the washer on a leaking tap, painting your sitting room or cleaning your windows rather than calling in the experts.

Take classes

Spend time learning new skills – perhaps an online course in home maintenance, a weekend gardening workshop or an evening class in cooking.

Enjoy becoming self-reliant

Embrace the feelings of satisfaction that will come from making things and solving problems yourself – from sourcing the ingredients or tools, reading instructions and taking advice through to actually completing the tasks. You'll feel proud that you can rely on yourself rather than always having to pay others to do everything for you.

DON'T DESPAIR IN THE FACE OF THE CLIMATE CRISIS

'Do your bit to combat the emergency'

It's understandable to feel helplessness and despair when thinking about the scale of the climate crisis. It's hard to feel otherwise when we are experiencing increasingly extreme weather events and scientists warn us that there's much worse to come.

That said, we mustn't allow ourselves to become so despondent and helpless that we give up and do nothing except grow angrier. Yes, it's good to tell the world how angry you are, but the ideal is to channel that anger into positive and proactive outlets and to have a mindset of wanting to make a difference.

By focusing on what you can do as an individual, you help offset your despair by taking concrete steps of reparation, such as lobbying for changes in the legislation or embracing lifestyle changes that reduce your carbon footprint.

Never dismiss your actions as too small or local – remember that throughout history some of humanity's biggest breakthroughs have come about only through the combined actions of individuals like you and me doing our bit.

Do what you can now to help, no matter how small.

Know your actions make a difference

Get out of the habit of justifying your choices by thinking you're only one person and saying things like, 'What does it matter if I use a plastic straw – it's only one?' or 'What difference does it really make to the world if I were to stop eating meat?' Understand that each one of our individual choices adds up to a very large whole – that when millions of us stop using plastic straws or eating meat, the global impact will be profound.

Ignore what others think

Let's imagine that you reduce your carbon footprint by no longer flying, turning vegan, buying mainly second-hand products, installing an air-source heat pump or buying an electric car. Given human nature, some of those around you will be sarcastic or critical about your choices. They'll make comments like 'Heat pumps are an expensive waste of money', 'Your electric car will leave you stranded with an empty battery' or 'Veganism is just a fad and you'll struggle to find fun foods to eat'. Well, just ignore them!

Whenever someone steps away and does something different, it's typical to see other people respond in this way and there's nothing you can do to change that. Simply ignore everything they say and remain focused on doing what you feel is the right thing to do.

Accept what you cannot change

Learn to accept changes that have already happened and which no one on earth can alter or reverse. For example, we're coming close to the planet reaching 1.5 degrees Celsius above pre-industrial-era averages, but no amount of demonstrations, lobbying and lifestyle changes can stop this happening. Be OK with this reality, knowing that all you can do is focus on reducing the chances of additional temperature increases and helping the growing numbers of people who will be adversely impacted in our warming world.

COLLECT MOMENTS, NOT OBJECTS

'Know that pleasure in things will quickly dwindle, but memories will endure.'

It's very easy to become focused on boosting our material wealth and possessions. Surrounded by relentless advertising and marketing campaigns, it's tempting to be forever updating our wardrobes, have the latest smartphone or TV, upgrading our car or investing in a new sofa. Being envious of what others possess (a topic explored in No. 22) doesn't help as it often compels us to buy things just to keep up with others.

The good news is that acquiring physical possessions isn't as fulfilling and meaningful as we imagine and at best brings us only short-term happiness. You only have to watch how quickly young children lose interest in their latest toys to realize how transient pleasure in our possessions can be.

True fulfilment comes from things we experience and that give us memories and lasting impressions – whether it's going on holidays and adventures, learning how to cook or paint, having cultural experiences or spending time with others. It's these experiences that have the power to energize and enrich our lives and to broaden our horizons and perspectives in ways that material possessions never can. It's through these that you'll open up your life to deeper levels of happiness and fulfilment.

Seeking experiences over material possessions brings you more fulfilment and joy.

When in doubt, choose experiences over things

When thinking of what to ask for at Christmas or for your birthday, suggest experiences every time – ask for something you've never tried before or one you really enjoyed and want to experience again (perhaps with your loved ones).

Take a similar approach when you're thinking of spending on yourself or on others. Before being tempted to buy another possession, question whether you really need that new jacket, car, TV or perfume. Try to focus your attention instead on selecting an exciting and new experience that you could give to yourself and/or your loved ones as a treat.

When walking around the shops or scrolling through online stores, avoid making impulse purchases just to make your day and to cheer you up. Instead, go to the theatre, cinema, beach or museum for a couple of hours – you'll feel much better and you'll have new memories to take home with you.

Document your experiences

Find a way of collecting your memories so that you can look back through them – to relive the enjoyable and positive feelings you had while paddling in the sea, visiting a theme park, viewing an art exhibition or learning how to ski.

The easiest way of revisiting our experiences is by taking photos and videos – something we do all the time. Just take care when sharing these with your friends and colleagues to avoid being seen as a show-off.

NOTHING LASTS

'Don't stress over what in a month or a year will be forgotten'

We take life far too seriously. In my coaching work, I find that so many of my clients allow their daily challenges to consume them – whether it's an obsessive determination to win and succeed or becoming engulfed by anxiety and stress when dealing with one problem after another.

We've all been there, becoming consumed by the need to achieve particular results, complete something, or overcome a problem as soon as possible. Today these issues and challenges may feel like the most important things in the world, but in the grand scheme of things we will remember very little about them in a month, year or decade from now.

Almost everything is transitory and impermanent and recognizing this truth can be cathartic. By stepping back from the minutiae of your daily life, you'll notice how fleeting your issues are and how quickly they fade over time. With this fresh perspective you're able to calm down and be less obsessed with what you achieve and instead focus on deciding how best to spend your time and energy.

If it won't matter in one year's time, why let it matter today?

Take the 'Will it matter in the future?' test

Each time you find yourself becoming consumed by an issue – whether positive or negative – pause to think through how much of your attention and concern you really need to invest. Ask yourself whether in a few years' time you or anyone else will even remember or care that today you ...

- gave up your evenings to become active in and elected as head of a local society
- sacrificed family time to impress your boss in order to win a promotion
- became stressed and ill trying to master a new skill or activity
- worked over the weekend to solve a work issue and missed out on watching your child's first dance performance.

Normally the answer will be no and this should be your cue to ease off putting so much pressure on yourself. Be less willing to become burnt out and give up what really matters, like family time, just to achieve something today that may be forgotten by next month.

Know that not everything is fleeting

There are exceptions to the rule that everything is temporary and will be forgotten in a few years' time. Learn to spot these exceptions and know that it's OK to become consumed by having to deal with them. Examples typically relate to your relationships and to your well-being, such as when someone close to you is very ill or dying, your marriage is struggling, or your reputation risks being damaged.

YOUR STORY'S NEVER OVER

'Never use age as an excuse to stop seeking fresh experiences'

Until your dying breath you have the potential to shape and define your life. It's your story and it's important to never give up on writing new chapters. Don't allow your thinking and beliefs or those of others tell you otherwise.

As we get older, many of us stop shaping the flow of our lives even when we have many years of active life ahead of us. We may feel we're no longer capable of achieving and creating, perhaps because of society's perception that once we've reached a certain age, our fate is predetermined and no longer in our hands.

This defeatist thinking is both wrong and unhealthy – by giving up on shaping our lives we're likely to age faster and die sooner. It's only through creating our own adventures and opening up new avenues that we remain energized and truly alive. In recognizing that our stories only finish on the day we die, we realize that age is only a number and that society's perceptions are just plain wrong.

No matter your age or situation, always keep working on your story, seeking whatever experiences, meaning and purpose you need to make your life's journey as fulfilling as possible.

If you're still breathing, then there's still time to pursue your dreams.

Put it into action

99

Break free of stereotypes

Challenge your preconceived thinking about getting old and what people should or shouldn't be doing in the later stages of their life. Get away from the common belief that being young is better and that youthful energy and ambition are best. Take a moment to observe the older people around you, take in what they're doing and achieving, and start appreciating them as simply slightly older versions of who you are today.

Keep your bucket list updated

Starting now, no matter your age, get into the habit of exploring new passions and activities. Experiencing new things will hopefully bring you joy, meaning and fulfilment. As each year passes and you're another year older, allow your dreams and goals to become ever more audacious, and always ignore what society thinks someone of your age should have on their bucket list! Reread No. 90 to be reminded of the benefits of doing crazy, crazy things.

F*CK OTHER PEOPLE'S ADVICE

'Take every tip with a pinch of salt, even mine!'

We spend our lives being given well-meaning advice – with tips from all sources, including family, friends, colleagues, social media feeds and coaches like myself. Occasionally, their suggestions are timely and helpful, but oftentimes they're not – either because they won't help you in this precise moment or will never help you at all.

Too much self-help wisdom is generic and conventional and not tailored to an individual's circumstances. The best option is to always treat other people's advice with a healthy dose of caution – taking some points on board that you feel might work for you while discarding most of what others want you to believe.

Just as you need to find your own unique path in life, you also need to develop your own self-help manual based on what works for you given your unique combination of experiences, background, personality, goals and challenges.

You are the best judge, so don't allow others to dictate what your life should look and feel like.

100

Develop your own self-help guide

Creating your own list of 'ways to win' is a journey in experimentation through repeated trial and error. To get started, go back through the other 99 entries in this book noting which pieces of advice feel helpful and useful. If you're not sure, add them to your list anyway for good measure (you can always review them later). Complete your list by adding any other self-help tips and suggestions you've previously tried and found useful.

On your list there'll be tips that are clearly very important for you and you should implement these now. Experiment with the remaining pieces of advice to discover whether they'll help you.

Through this process of trial and error, you'll begin to learn which advice works. When something doesn't, remove it from your list. Very quickly you'll end up with an individualized self-help guide to 'ways to win' that work for you.

AND FINALLY ...

'Now go off and turn the rest of your life into an amazing story!'

I sincerely hope that this book's 100 ways to win will be your launch pad for creating an extraordinary and fulfilling life.

Follow me online to continue being inspired by my insights and suggestions.

In addition, I'd really love to keep in touch with you and to hear how this book has energized you towards success. Feel free to connect with me on LinkedIn or to drop me an email – nigelcumberland@gmail.com

Would you like your people to read this book?

If you would like to discuss how you could bring these ideas to your team, we would love to hear from you. Our titles are available at competitive discounts when purchased in bulk across both physical and digital formats. We can offer bespoke editions featuring corporate logos, customized covers, or letters from company directors in the front matter can also be created in line with your special requirements.

We work closely with leading experts and organizations to bring forward-thinking ideas to a global audience. Our books are designed to help you be more successful in work and life.

For further information, or to request a catalogue, please contact: **jmbusiness@johnmurraypress.co.uk**

John Murray Business is an imprint of John Murray Press.

Unlock your full potential with Nigel Cumberland's

***100 Things* series**

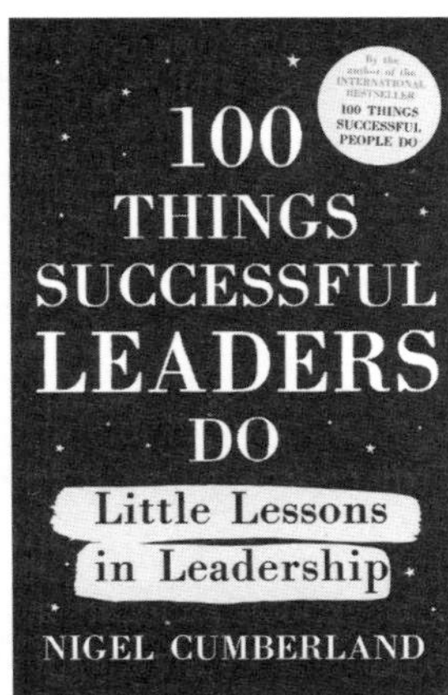